FLOYD CLYMER'S MOTORCYCLIST'S LIBRARY

The Book of the
A.J.S.

A PRACTICAL GUIDE ON THE HANDLING AND MAINTENANCE OF ALL 1955-65 A.J.S. 350 c.c. AND 500 c.c. O.H.V. TOURING SINGLES (EXCEPT MODELS 8 AND 14) AND 1965 NORTON MODELS 50 AND ES2

BY

W. C. HAYCRAFT
F.R.S.A.

ANNOUNCEMENT

By special arrangement with the original publishers of this book, Sir Isaac Pitman & Son, Ltd., of London, England, we have secured the exclusive publishing rights for this book, as well as all others in THE MOTORCYCLIST'S LIBRARY.

Included in THE MOTORCYCLIST'S LIBRARY are complete instruction manuals covering the care and operation of respective motorcycles and engines; valuable data on speed tuning, and thrilling accounts of motorcycle race events. See listing of available titles elsewhere in this edition.

We consider it a privilege to be able to offer so many fine titles to our customers.

FLOYD CLYMER
Publisher of Books Pertaining to Automobiles and Motorcycles

2125 W. PICO ST.   LOS ANGELES 6, CALIF.

INTRODUCTION

Welcome to the world of digital publishing ~ the book you now hold in your hand, while unchanged from the original edition, was printed using the latest state of the art digital technology. The advent of print-on-demand has forever changed the publishing process, never has information been so accessible and it is our hope that this book serves your informational needs for years to come. If this is your first exposure to digital publishing, we hope that you are pleased with the results. Many more titles of interest to the classic automobile and motorcycle enthusiast, collector and restorer are available via our website at www.VelocePress.com. We hope that you find this title as interesting as we do.

NOTE FROM THE PUBLISHER

The information presented is true and complete to the best of our knowledge. All recommendations are made without any guarantees on the part of the author or the publisher, who also disclaim all liability incurred with the use of this information.

TRADEMARKS

We recognize that some words, model names and designations, for example, mentioned herein are the property of the trademark holder. We use them for identification purposes only. This is not an official publication.

INFORMATION ON THE USE OF THIS PUBLICATION

This manual is an invaluable resource for the classic motorcycle enthusiast and a "must have" for owners interested in performing their own maintenance. However, in today's information age we are constantly subject to changes in common practice, new technology, availability of improved materials and increased awareness of chemical toxicity. As such, it is advised that the user consult with an experienced professional prior to undertaking any procedure described herein. While every care has been taken to ensure correctness of information, it is obviously not possible to guarantee complete freedom from errors or omissions or to accept liability arising from such errors or omissions. Therefore, any individual that uses the information contained within, or elects to perform or participate in do-it-yourself repairs or modifications acknowledges that there is a risk factor involved and that the publisher or its associates cannot be held responsible for personal injury or property damage resulting from the use of the information or the outcome of such procedures.

WARNING!

One final word of advice, this publication is intended to be used as a reference guide, and when in doubt the reader should consult with a qualified technician.

PREFACE

TODAY A.J.S. and Norton motor-cycles have a world-wide reputation for high performance, mechanical quietness, reliability, and economical running. Appearance and general finish too are excellent.

It has always been, and still is, the policy of Matchless Motor Cycles, Ltd., the makers of A.J.S. machines, of Plumstead Road, London, S.E.18, to develop and perfect their machines gradually, and to embody in the standard touring models their experience gained through participation in racing *and* trials events. 1964–5 improvements include the fitting of a gear-type oil pump, highly efficient "Roadholder" front forks, and new front and quickly-detachable rear wheels with light-alloy hubs and journal ball bearings. A.J.S. performance has thereby been still further improved.

As hitherto, the object of this handbook is to help *you* to obtain the maximum pleasure, mileage, m.p.h., m.p.g., and m.p.£ from your mount, and to reduce depreciation to the minimum.

If you have never before handled an A.J.S. or Norton, turn direct to Chapter I which deals with preliminaries, starting-up, gear changing, running-in, etc. Read and thoroughly digest the latest edition of the *Highway Code*. I also recommend the wearing of a crash helmet. Chapters II–V deal comprehensively with the correct *maintenance* of the following four-stroke O.H.V. single-cylinder touring models—
 1. The 1955–65 348 c.c. A.J.S. Models 16, 16S.
 2. The 1955–65 498 c.c. A.J.S. Models 18, 18S.
 3. The 1965 348 c.c. Norton Model 50 Mk. II.
 4. The 1965 498 c.c. Norton Model ES2 Mk. II.

The A.J.S. Models 16 and 18 are alternatively referred to as the "Sceptre" and "Statesman" respectively. The 1965 Norton Models 50 and ES2, by the way, are quite different from the 1955–63 Norton Models 50 and ES2 whose maintenance is comprehensively dealt with in *The Book of the Norton*, published by Pitmans. Except for their tank badges they are identical to the 1964–5 348 c.c. and 498 c.c. A.J.S. models.

All A.J.S. instructions in this handbook dated up to 1965 apply also to the corresponding 1965 Norton models. All A.J.S. instructions not dated are applicable to 1955–65 A.J.S. models and the 1965 Nortons specified above.

In conclusion I thank Matchless Motor Cycles, Ltd. of Plumstead, and Amal, Ltd. and Joseph Lucas, Ltd. of Birmingham, for their much appreciated assistance in providing technical data, and for according me permission to reproduce many excellent copyright illustrations.

W.C.H.

CONTENTS

CHAP. | | PAGE

I. HANDLING AN A.J.S. 1
Essential preliminaries—Starting up the engine—Gear changing—General driving hints

II. ALL ABOUT CARBURATION 11
Amal "Monobloc" carburettor—Carburettor maintenance—The air filter

III. THE LIGHTING SYSTEM 20
Illumination—Maintenance of battery—Maintenance of dynamo (1955–7)—The alternator and rectifier (1958–65)—The horn—The wiring system

IV. CORRECT LUBRICATION 39
Engine lubrication—Motor-cycle lubrication

V. GENERAL MAINTENANCE 58
Engine maintenance—Sparking plugs, contact-breaker, etc.—Timing the magneto (1955–7) Timing the ignition (1958–65)—Tappet adjustment—Decarbonizing and valve grinding—Valve timing—Motor-cycle maintenance—Tyre pressures—Wheel alignment—Brakes—The transmission—Steering head and suspension—Front and rear wheels

Index 125

CHAPTER 1

HANDLING AN A.J.S.

An A.J.S. O.H.V. single is easy to handle, and even the absolute novice quickly acquires confidence in the saddle. Beware, however, that you do not indulge in big throttle openings *until you have had ample road experience*. Also do not forget to follow the advice given in the *Highway Code*.

Essential Preliminaries. Before you can legally ride on the road—
(1) Insure against all *third-party* risks and obtain the vital "certificate of insurance." With a new machine you cannot get this until the machine is licensed, and an insurance "cover note" must be obtained. If you have a valuable machine, you are advised to take out full comprehensive insurance.

(2) Obtain the registration licence and registration book (Form R.F. I/2)* or renew the licence (Form R.F. I/A). Models 16 and 18 are taxed at the rate of £8 per annum (the same if a sidecar is attached). The licence disc must be prominently displayed in a waterproof and transparent holder at the forward end of the machine.

(3) Obtain a six months "provisional" or a "full" driving licence (Form D.L.1). This is valid for three years. The cost of a "provisional" or "full" licence is 10s. or 15s. respectively.

(4) Check that the headlamp-mounted Smith speedometer is in proper working order. It must indicate within ± 10 per cent accuracy when 30 m.p.h. is being exceeded, and it must be illuminated at night so that the dial is readily readable.

(5) If you carry a pillion-passenger, see that he or she holds a current three-year driving licence for Group G if you are a "learner."

(6) If you are ineligible for a "full" driving licence, attach "L" plates to the front and back of the machine.

(7) Verify that the rear lamp shines red to the rear and clearly illuminates the rear number plate letters and figures with a white light. The lamp and number plate must be clean.

(8) If the machine is second-hand make sure that it is thoroughly roadworthy. It is now an offence to ride an unroadworthy machine on the road. Check that the tyres have good treads and that the steering, lights, and brakes are fully efficient. Also see that the horn gives "audible warning of approach."

* The A.J.S. engine and frame numbers required on Form R.F. I/2 will be found on the near-side of the crankcase and the off-side of the saddle lug, or on the main frame head lug (1958–65).

All the official forms referred to above may be obtained from any money-order post office.

You are not eligible for a three-year driving licence for Group G *unless* you are 16 and have complied with one of these conditions—

(*a*) You have held a licence (other than a provisional or Visitor's

Fig. 1. A Flexible and Fast Tourer with Clean Lines and Mechanical Quietness—The 1965 Sceptre (Model 16)

The 500 c.c. Statesman (Model 18) is very similar to the 350 c.c. model illustrated. Both these modern push-rod O.H.V. singles are light, easy to handle, have a good turn of speed, snappy acceleration, and a low fuel consumption. 1964–5 improvements include a most efficient gear-type oil pump, "Roadholder" front forks, and new hubs and brakes. Riding comfort has been very closely studied and Dolphin fairings are listed as optional extras.

licence) authorizing the driving of vehicles of the class or description applied for within a period of ten years ending on the date of coming into force of the licence applied for.

(*b*) You have passed the prescribed driving test (this includes a test passed while serving in H.M. Forces) during the said period of ten years.

Is the Riding Position Comfortable? To enjoy motor-cycling it is essential that the riding position is comfortable. The handlebar controls, the footrests, the rear-brake pedal, and the foot gear-change lever are adjustable for position.

STARTING THE ENGINE

First verify that there is sufficient petrol and oil in the tanks. Handlebar controls are shown in Fig. 2; oil tank and gearbox replenishment are dealt with on pages 44 and 49 respectively. Check that the gear-change pedal *is* in neutral (*see* Figs. 4, 5).

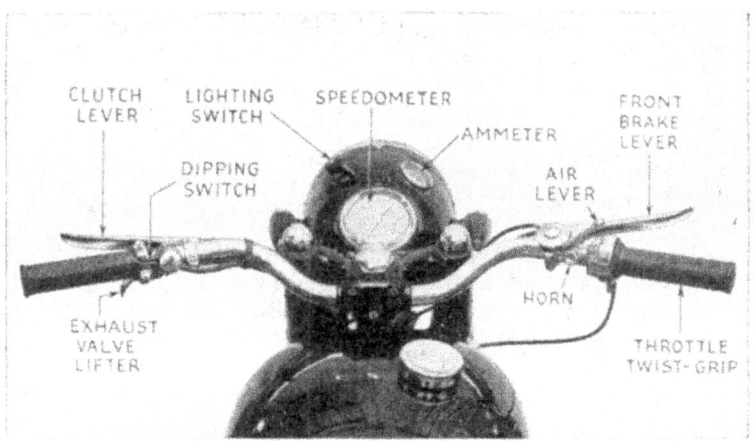

Fig. 2. Layout of Handlebar Controls (1954 Onwards)

All controls are adjustable for angle and are operated by inward movement. 1956–60 models have a combined dipping-switch and horn push and 1958–61 models have an ignition key in the centre of the lighting switch. On 1962–5 models two switches are provided on the headlamp. The ignition switch is the right-hand one.

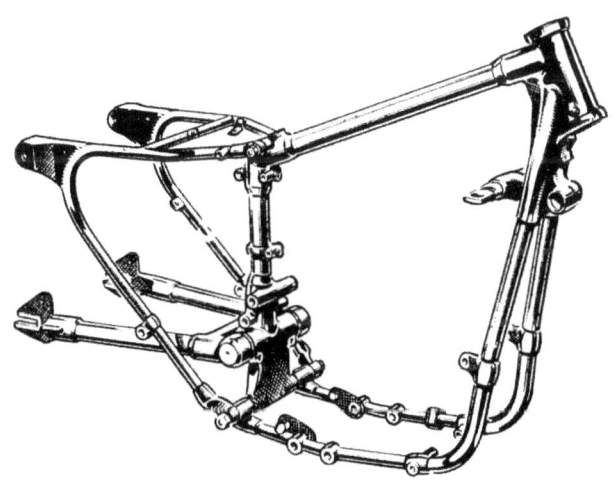

Fig. 3. The 1960–5 350 c.c. and 500 c.c. Models have a Duplex Heavyweight Frame with Twin Front Down Tubes
(*By courtesy of "Motor Cycling"*)

Adjusting the Controls. If the engine is cold—
(1) Set the throttle so that it is slightly open by turning the twist-grip *inwards* about *one-sixth* of its total movement.
(2) Completely close the air-control lever.
(3) Turn the ignition switch on 1958–65 models to the "ON" position.
(4) Fully advance the ignition-control lever (where fitted) by pushing it *outward* to its *full extent*, and then retard it by about *two-fifths* of its total movement by pulling it *inwards*.

If the engine is already warm, open the throttle about a quarter and the air-control lever half to three-quarters.

The Petrol Tank Filler Cap. Some riders find that the filler cap does not come away instantly. On A.J.S. machines, to release the filler cap quickly, depress it slightly, then turn it fully anti-clockwise and withdraw the cap. It has two locking positions.

Main and Reserve Petrol Taps. Some A.J.S. singles have down-draught type Amal carburettors and on such machines it is important when leaving a machine standing for more than a few minutes always to turn off both the main and reserve-supply petrol taps.

Both taps are of the horizontal-plunger type. As mentioned in a later paragraph, it is advisable normally to run with only the off-side tap open. Refuelling should be undertaken as soon as possible after being forced to draw upon the reserve fuel supply. The reserve supply tap should then be shut immediately. On 1955 and later models, to close either tap, push the plunger right in; to open it, pull the plunger right out.

If Engine is Cold. If the engine (especially a new one) is stone cold, it is generally advisable to free the piston before attempting to start up. Raise the exhaust-valve lifter and kick the engine over smartly about three times.

Starting Procedure. After setting the controls, depress the float chamber "tickler" momentarily, but do not flood the carburettor so that petrol drips from it. It is assumed that the petrol has been turned on by using the *off-side* tap. Use the other to maintain a reserve supply.

Turn the engine over slowly with the kick-starter pedal until the resistance of compression is felt. Raise the exhaust-valve lifter and allow the piston just to pass the position of full compression. Then allow the kick-starter pedal to return almost to its normal position.

Release the exhaust-valve lifter and simultaneously kick the engine over sharply with a long swinging kick. If nothing happens, repeat the procedure until something does! When the engine fires, fully open the air-control lever slowly, advance the ignition lever (where fitted) fully, and open the throttle slightly to make the engine run at a moderate speed on the pilot jet. Check the oil circulation (*see* page 45).

Emergency Starting (1958-65 A.J.S. Models). On the coil-ignition models the ignition switch has an emergency starting position. Should the battery for some reason become badly discharged, turn the ignition switch to the "EMG" position. This connects the alternator direct to the ignition coil and enables the engine to be started independently of the battery. Immediately the engine starts turn the ignition switch to the "IGN" position, otherwise misfiring will develop.

Excessive Flooding is Risky. Do not adopt the pernicious habit of swamping the carburettor with petrol before starting up. Such flooding incurs a grave risk of neat petrol entering the cylinder from a downdraught carburettor and destroying the vital oil film between the piston and cylinder. Dripping petrol also causes a slight fire risk.

If Engine Refuses to Start. If the engine refuses to start at the third kick, verify that petrol is reaching the float chamber by depressing the tickler. When you are satisfied on this point, remove and carefully inspect the sparking plug. Clean the plug, check its gap, and replace it (*see* pages 61-3).

Correct Method of Warming Up. Do not race the engine immediately after starting up from cold, as it takes some time for the oil to circulate properly. Running the engine too fast also generates excessive heat. On the other hand, do not warm up the engine too slowly, or the pump will not work fast enough to circulate the oil properly and the combustion of a rather cold mixture will be incomplete, with the result that condensation on and corrosion of the cylinder walls may occur. Never allow the engine to idle for long, especially in hot weather, and do not travel fast until the oil has warmed up.

Speedometer Readings. The top set of figures on the dial records the total mileage and automatically returns to zero when 100,000 miles is recorded. The bottom set of figures records the mileage since the trip was set to zero, and the red figures indicate tenths of a mile. It is a good plan to set the trip to zero before driving off on each run. To do this, pull and turn to the *right* the knob (protruding from the lower part of the speedometer unit) until "000·0" appears.

GEAR CHANGING

Ease the A.J.S. off its stand, with the engine ticking over and the foot gear-change pedal in neutral, sit astride the machine, and disengage the clutch, using the handlebar lever (*see* Fig. 2).

Engaging First Gear. Raise the foot gear-change pedal *fully* with the toe of the foot and engage first (bottom) gear (*see* Figs. 4, 5). Slight backward or forward movement of the machine often facilitates engagement. As soon as first gear is *felt* to engage, remove the toe from the pedal.

If difficulty is experienced in engaging first gear, wait a few seconds before making another attempt. Initial difficulty in engaging first gear on a *new* machine usually cures itself quite soon, and sticking clutch-plates can be rectified by stopping the engine (by raising the exhaust-valve lifter)

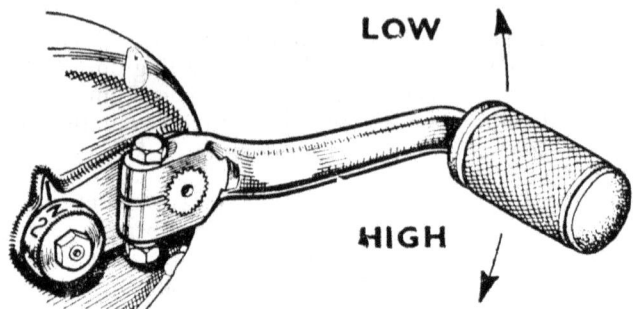

FIG. 4. THE FOOT GEAR-CHANGE INDICATOR (1955–6, 1958–65)
The indicator itself comprises a small drum having the gear positions marked as shown. *N* (neutral) is shown aligned with the dash mark on the gearbox shell.

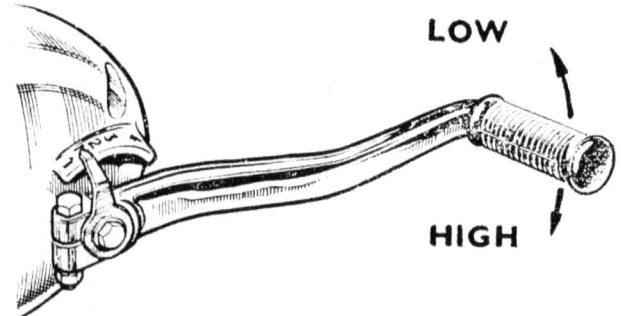

FIG. 5. THE FOOT GEAR-CHANGE INDICATOR (1957 MODELS)
The indicator comprises a pointer on the gear-change lever shaft, and a marked quadrant on the gearbox.

and smartly operating the kick-starter several times with the clutch fully disengaged.

To Move Off. Having engaged first gear, move off by slowly releasing the clutch lever. As the machine gathers speed and the engine takes the full load, gradually increase the throttle opening by means of the twist-grip, so as to maintain a progressive rise in the speed of the engine and machine.

Changing Up (First to Second). As soon as your A.J.S. has reached a speed of about fifteen m.p.h. in first gear, change up into second gear. Once again disengage the clutch, slightly close the throttle, pause a second, and then *depress* the gear-change pedal to its *full extent* with the toe, until second gear is *felt* to engage perfectly. Then engage the clutch and also remove the toe from the pedal to allow the pedal to return to its normal horizontal position.

Changing Up (to Third and Fourth). Progressively increase the throttle opening until the machine has plenty of momentum. Now disengage the clutch, throttle down slightly, pause a second, and then smartly, but without force, *depress* the gear-change pedal fully until third gear is *felt* to engage perfectly. Engage the clutch, remove the toe from the pedal, and throttle up to maintain a good road speed without any tendency for the engine to "knock." To change into fourth (i.e. top gear) repeat the procedure with the machine travelling quite fast.

To Change Down (Fourth to Third). Throttle down to a normal speed for third gear. Disengage the clutch, throttle up slightly, pause a second, and *raise* the gear-change pedal to its *full extent* with the toe of the foot until third gear is *felt* to engage. Immediately afterwards engage the clutch, remove the toe from the pedal, and throttle up to compensate for the increase in the speed of the engine relative to rear-wheel speed.

To Change Down (to Second and First). The required procedure is similar to that just described for changing down from fourth to third gear. With the toe of the foot *raise* the gear-change pedal to its *full extent* during each gear change. Each full movement of the pedal engages the *next* gear in the gear-change sequence as shown by the indicator in Figs. 4, 5.

To change from fourth or third gear into first (bottom) gear, it is not *essential* to complete the full gear-changing procedure for each intermediate gear, although this should be done when hill climbing. The method which can be used is to bring the machine to a crawl by means of the throttle and brakes, disengage the clutch, and then raise the gear-change pedal to its *full extent*—three times or twice (in quick succession), according to whether top or third gear was previously engaged. Each time you raise the gear-change pedal "blip" the engine, i.e. throttle up slightly. Then gently re-engage the clutch.

Silence Is Golden. Noisy gear changing is bad for sensitive ears, and worse still for the gearbox! Learn to change gear silently. Here are a few golden rules—

(1) Make full use of the four gear-ratios provided. The gear-change pedal always returns to the same position, but do not forget where it is.

(2) Do not "bully" the machine up a steep incline in top gear.

(3) Change gear *before* your mount gets "hot and bothered."
(4) Use a nicely co-ordinated and almost simultaneous movement when operating the clutch, throttle, and gear-change pedal.
(5) Keep a steady pressure on the gear-change pedal and hold the clutch out *until the gear is felt to engage.* At other times remove the foot.
(6) Do not race the engine in the lower gears to "impress the lads." They may like it (perhaps) but your engine will hate you!
(7) Be kind to the gearbox and give it its oil ration occasionally (*see* page 49).

GENERAL DRIVING HINTS

Negotiating Hills. Your A.J.S. will romp up gentle gradients, but maintain the engine r.p.m. high by making full use of the gearbox where

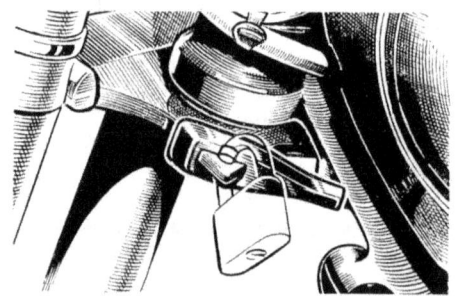

FIG. 6. TO PREVENT THEFT USE AN A.J.S. LOCKING BAR AND PADLOCK TO SECURE THE FRONT FORKS

The locking bar is an inexpensive optional extra (Part No. 018691) and can be fitted to most 1955–65 models. Other optional extras include a rear chain case, pannier frames and bags, and crash bar sets.

necessary and *in good time.* On no account permit the engine to labour. Be liberal with the throttle opening, and do not retard the ignition-control lever (where fitted) unless this is essential (to ward off a "knock"), as this reduces power output.

When descending steep hills, open the air lever wide and close the throttle. This will not only cool the engine, but it will engage engine compression to exert a powerful braking effect.

Use of Brakes. Acquire the habit of using *both* brakes simultaneously, as this gives powerful braking with minimum and even wear of the brake linings and tyres.

Excessive and fierce brake application plays havoc with the tyres and transmission, and for this reason you should learn to *drive on the throttle* and use the brakes as little and as seldom as possible. Make use of engine

HANDLING AN A.J.S. 9

compression as a brake when descending hills (*see* previous paragraph), but never use the clutch, ignition switch (1958–65), or exhaust-valve lifter for controlling speed. This places a motor-cyclist beyond the pale.

To Stop the Machine. To effect a normal stop on the road use the following procedure—
(1) Close the throttle by means of the twist-grip.
(2) Fully disengage the clutch.
(3) Apply *both* brakes simultaneously, increasing the hand and foot pressure as the brakes take effect.
(4) Raise the gear-change pedal fully once or several times (according to which gear is already engaged) until you get into first gear. Then depress the pedal *very slightly* with the toe until "neutral" (*see* Figs. 4, 5) is obtained.
(5) Engage the clutch by gently releasing the lever.

To Stop the Engine. After bringing the motor-cycle to a halt with the throttle closed (as far as the throttle-stop permits*), it is only necessary to raise the exhaust-valve lifter for a few seconds in order to extinguish all signs of life. On 1958–65 models it is not necessary to use the exhaust-valve lifter; just turn the ignition key to the centre. Before you leave your machine, turn off the petrol tap to prevent accidental "flooding."

Running-in New Machine. On covering 1,000 miles it is not harmful to step up the speed of a *new* machine gradually, but refrain from using full throttle until about 2,000 miles have been covered. A new A.J.S. must be properly run-in, or it may be permanently spoiled. Here is some sound advice—
(1) Don't exceed one-third full throttle for 1,000 miles.
(2) Don't "over-rev" the engine when idling or on the road, especially in the lower gears.
(3) Don't often exceed 30 m.p.h. in top gear.
(4) Don't permit the engine to labour or "knock." Change down in good time when hill climbing.
(5) Don't run the engine with the machine stationary for more than a minute or two.
(6) Don't forget to keep the engine, gearbox, and machine correctly lubricated (*see* Chapter IV).

After Covering 400–500 Miles. A certain amount of bedding-down occurs, and it is important to check the adjustment of the following: (*a*) tappets, (*b*) contact-breaker points, (*c*) steering-head bearings, (*d*) primary and secondary chains, and (*e*) brakes. Steering-head bearing

* The correct throttle-stop setting is such that when the engine is warmed up and the throttle is closed, the engine ticks over smoothly (*see* page 14).

adjustment is very important, as slack bearings will suffer. After the initial bedding-down and necessary adjustments have been made, further adjustment is needed much less frequently.

The A.J.S. Free Service Scheme. Every owner of a brand new A.J.S. is entitled to *one* free service and inspection after covering 500 miles, or, at the latest, *three months* after taking delivery. It is an excellent plan to take advantage of this free service and inspection, as about 20 important maintenance points are carefully attended to.

Every new machine has a free service voucher supplied in the tool box and the voucher should be handed to the dealer from whom you bought the machine. He will then check over and where necessary attend to your mount. A charge is, of course, made for oils and greases used.

Colloidal Graphite Beneficial for Running-in. It is beneficial during the running-in period to mix *one pint* of Acheson's Colloidal Graphite with each *gallon of engine oil*. This benefits the cylinder and bearing surfaces. If the compound (obtainable from most garages) is used after running-in, reduce the amount by one half.

Advice on Avoiding Accidents. Accidents on the road occur atrociously often. Below is some sound practical advice.

(1) Wear a crash helmet. A fractured skull and severe concussion can cause a shocking "hangover" for a long period and can easily be fatal.

(2) Do not speed on major roads, or apparently major roads, having minor cross-roads. This can lead to being rammed at right-angles.

(3) Exercise special care at cross-roads and roundabouts.

(4) Keep a good distance behind car drivers.

(5) Always give *clear* hand signals in *ample* time.

(6) Do not cut in or indulge in "stunt" riding.

(7) Never apply the brakes fiercely on wet roads.

(8) Keep a close watch when approaching pedestrian crossings and passing stationary cars near the kerb.

(9) Avoid approaching traffic lights too fast.

(10) Do not become over-confident and ride excessively fast.

(11) Never ride fast in foggy weather.

CHAPTER II

ALL ABOUT CARBURATION

ALL 1955–65 single-cylinder 350 c.c. and 500 c.c. A.J.S. engines have a "Monobloc" type Amal needle-jet carburettor fitted.

AMAL "MONOBLOC" CARBURETTOR

The Amal "Monobloc" carburettor specified on all 1955 and later A.J.S. O.H.V. singles differs from the earlier type, used before 1955, in several respects. But its general functioning is similar. The "Monobloc" design includes: a horizontal float chamber made integral with the carburettor body; a float needle of moulded nylon; a top petrol-feed; a needle jet with bleed holes giving two-way compensation; and a detachable pilot jet which can be easily cleaned.

Fig. 7 shows all the essential parts of the instrument. The float chamber (13) and needle (9) maintain a constant level of petrol in the needle jet (14) and the pilot jet (17). The selection by the makers of the appropriate jet sizes and main-bore choke ensures a proper atomizing and proportioning of the petrol and air sucked into the engine.

The air valve (3) is normally kept fully raised, and the throttle valve (24) controlled by the handlebar twist-grip controls the volume of mixture, and therefore the power. At all throttle openings a correct mixture is automatically obtained.

The "Monobloc" carburettor, like the former instrument, operates in four stages. When opening the throttle from the fully closed position to one-eighth open (for tick-over) the mixture is supplied by the pilot jet (17), and the strength of the mixture is determined by the setting of the knurled pilot-air adjusting screw (20) which has a coil locking-spring to facilitate adjustment. As the throttle is opened slightly farther, the main jet system comes into action, the mixture being augmented by the main jet (16) through the pilot by-pass.

The amount of cut-away on the atmospheric side of the throttle valve regulates the petrol-to-air ratio between one-eighth and one-quarter throttle. The needle jet (14) and the jet needle (23) take over the mixture regulation between one-quarter and three-quarter throttle, and the mixture strength is determined by the relative position of the needle in the clip (4) attached to the throttle valve (24). When the throttle is opened beyond three-quarters, the mixture strength is determined only by the size of the main jet. Note that the main jet (16) does not spray petrol direct

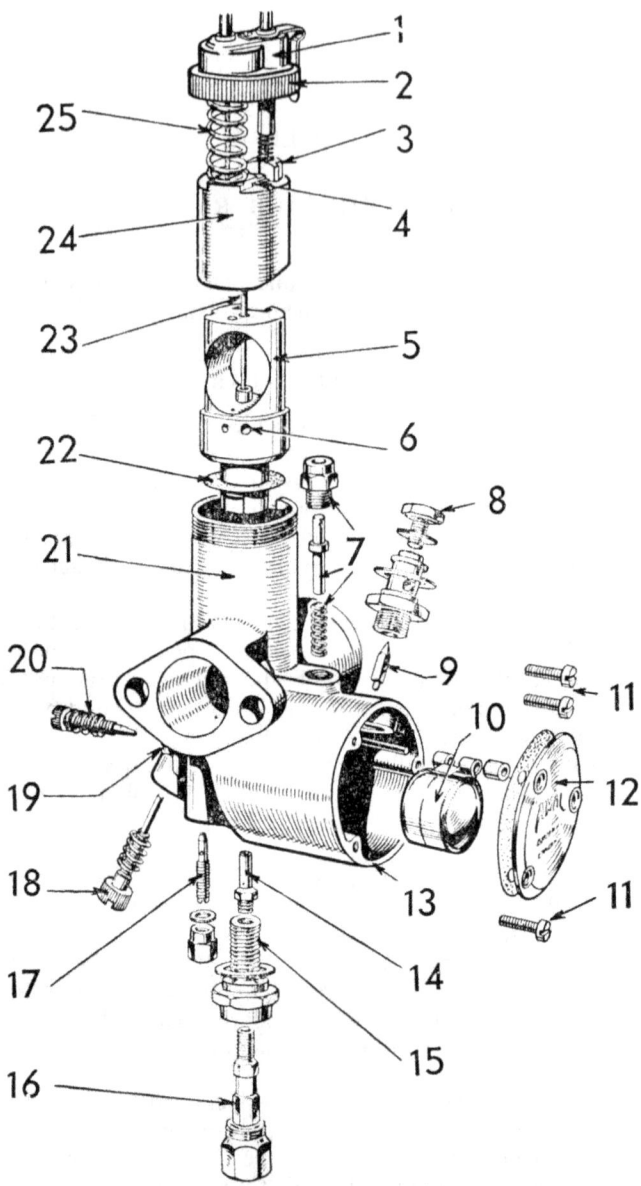

Fig. 7. Amal "Monobloc" Carburettor (1955 Onwards) Shown Dismantled

(*By courtesy of B.S.A. Motor Cycles, Ltd.*)

12

into the carburettor mixing chamber, but discharges through the needle jet into the primary air-chamber. From there it enters the main choke through the primary air-choke. The latter has a two-way compensating action in conjunction with the "bleed" holes in the needle jet. Pilot and

TABLE I
AMAL CARBURETTOR SETTINGS FOR 1955-6 SINGLES

Model	Main Jet	Pilot Jet	Throttle Valve	Needle Position
350 c.c. O.H.V. (no air filter)	210	30	376/3	3
350 c.c. O.H.V. (with air filter)	200	30	376/3	3
500 c.c. O.H.V. (to engine 27000)	240	30	376/3	2
500 c.c. O.H.V. (after No. 27000)	260	30	389/3	3

main jet behaviour are not affected by this two-way compensation which governs only acceleration at normal cruising speed.

TUNING AMAL "MONOBLOC" CARBURETTOR

Normally *it is unwise to interfere with the maker's carburettor setting (see* Tables I–III) unless there is a very special reason for doing so. However, it is sometimes desirable to make a slow-running adjustment with the pilot adjusting-screw and throttle-stop screw.

KEY TO FIG. 7

1. Mixing-chamber cap.
2. Mixing-chamber lock ring.
3. Air valve.
4. Jet-needle clip.
5. Jet block.
6. Air passage to pilot jet.
7. Tickler assembly.
8. Banjo securing-bolt.
9. Float needle.
10. Float.
11. Float-chamber cover screws.
12. Float-chamber cover.
13. Float chamber.
14. Needle jet.
15. Main-jet holder.
16. Main jet.
17. Pilot jet.
18. Throttle-stop adjusting screw.
19. Jet-block locating screw.
20. Pilot-air adjusting screw.
21. Mixing chamber.
22. Fibre seal.
23. Jet needle.
24. Throttle valve.
25. Throttle return-spring.

THE BOOK OF THE A.J.S.

Table II

AMAL CARBURETTOR SETTINGS FOR 1957–61 SINGLES

Model (No air filter)	Main Jet	Pilot Jet	Throttle Valve	Needle Position
350 c.c. O.H.V.	220*	30	376/3½	3
500 c.c. O.H.V.	260*	30	389/3½	3

* On 1958–61 350 c.c. models the correct main jet size is 210. Where an air filter is fitted, reduce the main jet size by 10. This applies to 1957–61 350 c.c. and 500 c.c. models.

Table III

AMAL CARBURETTOR SETTINGS FOR 1962–5 SINGLES

Model	Main Jet	Pilot Jet	Throttle Valve	Needle Position
350 c.c. O.H.V. (1962–3)	230	25	3½	3
500 c.c. O.H.V.	300	25	3½	3
350 c.c. O.H.V. (1964–5)	260	25	3	3
500 c.c. O.H.V. (1964–5)	290	25	3½	3

To vary the strength of the running mixture (rarely necessary), it is necessary to adjust the height of the needle in the throttle valve, or else to fit a larger or smaller size main jet. The condition of the sparking plug will provide an excellent guide to the condition of the mixture. A sooty plug indicates an over-rich mixture.

To Make a Slow-running Adjustment. This should be effected with the engine already *warmed up*. If the adjustment is appreciably at fault, screw home the pilot-air adjusting screw fully and then unscrew it (usually about two complete turns) until the engine idles at an excessive speed, with the throttle twist-grip closed and the throttle slide abutting the throttle-stop screw. The air lever should be fully open and the ignition lever (where automatic ignition-advance is not provided) should be set to obtain the best slow-running (half to two-thirds advanced).

Unscrew the throttle-stop screw until the engine slows up and begins to falter. Then screw the pilot-air adjusting screw in or out as required to enable the engine to run regularly and faster. To weaken the mixture, screw the pilot-air adjusting screw *outwards*.

Slowly lower the throttle-stop screw until the engine again begins to falter. Then reset the pilot-air adjusting screw to obtain the best slow-running. If after making this second adjustment the engine ticks over too fast, repeat the adjustment a third time. The combined adjustment sounds complicated but in practice is quite simple. It is important to avoid excessive richness of the slow-running mixture, especially if much riding is done on small throttle openings; if the mixture is too rich, considerable running on the pilot jet will occur while riding, with consequently a high fuel consumption.

Aim at obtaining the best tick-over, preferably on a mixture just bordering on the weak side. The engine should be on the point of spitting-back.*

Obstructed Pilot Jet. If the adjustment of the pilot jet does not obtain the desired results and the engine will not idle nicely with the throttle almost closed, the air lever fully open, and the ignition lever (where fitted) half to two-thirds advanced, it is possible that the pilot jet is obstructed. The jet passage is very small and can readily become choked.

With the "Monobloc" carburettor (*see* Fig. 7) to remove the pilot jet (17), remove the pilot jet cover-nut and then unscrew the jet itself which should be thoroughly cleaned in petrol and then blown through. See that the air passage (6) to the pilot jet, and also the pilot outlet, are quite clear.

Bad Slow-running. If it is found impossible to obtain good slow-running by making the pilot-air adjustment as described on page 14, it is probable that some defect other than carburation is responsible for preventing the engine running smoothly at low revolutions. Air leaks or badly-seating valves may weaken the mixture. Defects in the ignition system may also be responsible for poor tick-over. The sparking plug may be oily, or the points set too close (*see* page 61). Possibly the spark is excessively advanced or the contact-breaker needs attention (*see* pages 63–5).

Also examine the h.t. cable for signs of shorting and check the tappet adjustment (*see* page 71).

Excessive Fuel Consumption. If in spite of careful checking on the tuning of the carburettor, high fuel consumption continues, it is likely that

---

* Rev the engine up and down sharply several times (while at rest and while riding) and note whether the exhaust is nice and crisp, with no "flat spots" as the twist-grip is turned. It is essential to combine good tick-over with good acceleration.

one or more of the under-mentioned causes is responsible for wastage of precious fuel. Late ignition timing will eat into your petrol supplies quickly. The same applies to poor engine compression due to badly-fitting piston rings or valves. Also take into consideration the question of flooding due to a faulty float, air leakage at the joint between the carburettor and the engine, weak valve springs. See that no wastage is caused by slack petrol pipe union-nuts or leakage from the float-chamber cover.

Twist-grip Adjustment. Adjustment should be such that the grip is free and easy to twist, but "stays put." The spring tension on the twist-grip rotating sleeve is regulated by a screw incorporated in one-half of the twist-grip body. To increase the tension, loosen the lock-nut and turn the screw into the body as required.

It is possible to move the complete twist-grip on the handlebars by slackening the two screws which clamp it in position. The best position of the twist-grip is that which gives the cleanest and straightest path to the throttle cable between the handlebars and the under-side of the petrol tank.

On some 1955 and later models a nipple is used for lubricating the throttle cable, and so ensures smooth throttle operation. If any stiffness or jerkiness occurs, inject a little engine oil through the nipple. When doing this, apply the gun as nearly vertically as possible, with the nozzle downwards.

CARBURETTOR MAINTENANCE

To ensure correct carburation it is advisable occasionally to remove the carburettor from the engine, strip it down completely, and then thoroughly clean it. It is a good plan to do this about every six months as described below.

Dismantling "Monobloc" Carburettor. Close both petrol taps and disconnect the twin petrol pipes by undoing the banjo bolt (8) over the float chamber (*see* Fig. 7). Referring to Fig. 7, unscrew the mixing-chamber knurled lock-ring (2) on top of the carburettor and remove the two nuts securing the carburettor flange to the face of the inlet port. Then remove the body of the carburettor (21), complete with the integral float chamber (13). While removing the carburettor, pull the air valve (3) and the throttle valve (24) from the mixing chamber and tie them up temporarily out of the way. It is rarely necessary to disconnect the slides from the cables. Check that the flange washer is sound.

Further dismantling is straightforward. Referring to Fig. 7, to remove the jet needle (23), withdraw the jet-needle clip (4) on top of the throttle valve, and remove the needle. To obtain access to the float (10), remove the three screws (11) securing the float-chamber cover (12). Lift out the hinged float (10) and withdraw the moulded-nylon needle (9). Lay both

ALL ABOUT CARBURATION 17

aside for cleaning. The float-chamber vent, by the way, is embodied in the tickler assembly (7), and the top-feed union houses a filter element of nylon which is rapidly accessible for cleaning.

To remove the main jet (16), remove the main-jet cover and unscrew the jet from the jet holder (15), which should also be unscrewed. Remove the jet-block locating screw (19) to the left of and slightly below the pilot-air adjusting screw. Then push or tap out the jet block (5) and fibre seal (22) through the large end of the mixing chamber (21). To remove the pilot jet (17), remove the pilot-jet cover nut and unscrew the jet.

To Clean the Carburettor. Wash all the carburettor components, thoroughly clean with petrol and blow through the various ducts and passages to make sure they are quite clear. Avoid using a fluffy rag for drying purposes. Pay special attention to the small pilot-jet passages in the jet block. See that all impurities are removed from inside the float chamber. On the "Monobloc" carburettor do not forget to clean the detachable pilot jet and the nylon filter inside the banjo for the petrol pipe unions.

Inspecting the Parts. When dismantling the carburettor it is advisable to make a close inspection of the various parts if the carburettor has been in continuous service for a considerable period.

1. THE FLOAT CHAMBER. Examine the components very carefully and check that the vent is unobstructed. The float must be in perfect condition. Clean the moulded-nylon needle on the "Monobloc" carburettor very thoroughly, and be careful not to damage it.

2. THE THROTTLE VALVE. Test this for fit in the mixing chamber. Should excessive play exist, renew the slide forthwith. See that the new slide has the correct amount of cut-away.

3. THE JET-NEEDLE CLIP. The spring clip securing the tapered needle to the throttle valve must grip the needle firmly, and free rotation must *not* occur, as this causes the needle groove to wear. Always be careful to replace the needle with the clip in the central groove.

4. THE JET BLOCK. Before tapping this home in the mixing chamber verify by blowing that the pilot-jet ducts are clear and that the jet-block fibre seal is in good condition.

5. THE CARBURETTOR FLANGE. Examine this for truth with a straight-edge. Distortion sometimes occurs, and this may cause an air leak. If the flange is slightly concave, file and rub down the face with emery cloth until it is dead flat and smooth. Alternatively have the face ground on a machine. If a rubber "O" ring is fitted, replace it if worn.

Wear of Jet Needle. The needle itself does *not* wear, though some wear of the groove may occur if the jet-needle clip is not grasping the needle firmly. If the mixture is too rich with the clip in No. 1 groove (nearest the top), it is probable that the jet needle needs to be renewed because of wear. It is assumed that the carburettor is correctly tuned and that no flooding occurs.

Assembling "Monobloc" Carburettor. Do this in the reverse order of dismantling. Referring to Fig. 7, screw home the pilot jet (17) and the pilot jet cover-nut, not omitting to replace its washer. Push or tap home the jet block (5) and fibre seal (22) through the large end of the mixing chamber (21). Check that the fibre seal fitted to the stub of the jet block is in good condition. Then fit the jet-block locating-screw (19). Screw the main-jet holder (15) into the jet block, after checking that the washer for the holder is sound. Next screw the main jet (16) into the jet holder.

Replace the moulded-nylon needle (9) in the float chamber (13), and fit the hinged float (10) with the *narrow* side of the hinge uppermost. Afterwards fit the float-chamber cover (12) and secure by means of the three screws (11). Verify that the cover and body faces are undamaged and quite clean. Renew the washer.

If previously removed, attach the jet needle (23) to the throttle valve (24) and secure with the jet-needle clip (4), making sure that the clip enters the central groove.

Position the carburettor-flange washer, and offer up the carburettor to the face of the inlet port after easing the air and throttle valves (3) and (24) down into the mixing chamber. When easing the throttle valve home, make sure that the tapered jet needle (23) really enters the hole in the jet block (5). Secure the carburettor flange firmly to the engine by means of the two nuts, and tighten these evenly. Tighten down firmly the mixing-chamber knurled lock-ring (2) and see that the throttle slide works freely when this is tightened down.

Finally reconnect the twin petrol pipes by tightening the banjo-securing bolt (8) over the float chamber (13).

THE AIR FILTER

Maintenance. An air filter of the "oil-wetted" type is fitted as an optional extra to A.J.S. models. In the United Kingdom the roads are excellent and the air comparatively free from dust, and it is questionable whether the fitting of an air filter, except for use abroad in countries where the roads are poor and dusty, will appreciably prolong the life of the cylinder and piston.

Where an air filter is fitted, it is advisable about every 2,500–5,000 miles according to road conditions, to withdraw the filter element; wash it thoroughly in petrol, paraffin, or other suitable solvent, and allow to dry. Then submerge the element completely for a few minutes in thin oil (SAE 20) of the type recommended on page 55 for the "Teledraulic" front forks. Remove the element, allow all surplus oil to drain off, and afterwards replace in the air-filter case. It is desirable to renew the filter element about every 10,000 miles.

To Remove Filter Element (1956–60 Models). First pull the rubber hose off the air-intake of the "Monobloc" carburettor after releasing the clip (1957). Next remove the frame cover and pull off the hose end from the air filter. Then remove the bolts which secure the air filter to the oil tank and remove the complete filter assembly. Note that the filter element is secured in its cage by bolts, nuts, and locking washers.

After cleaning the filter (*see* a previous paragraph), replace it. When replacing the hose on the filter, see that it is properly located. The end of the rubber hose is split along the edge of the lip, and it is important to make sure that the neck of the filter assembly enters this groove.

To Remove Filter Element (1961–4 Models). First remove the top pivot bolt. Also remove the bottom nut on the filter. Then remove the filter with hose. The filter compartment can now be separated to gain access to the filter element. Maintenance should be effected as described in a previous paragraph.

CHAPTER III

THE LIGHTING SYSTEM

To ensure maximum illumination from the lamps at all times, a little attention to the equipment is normally necessary and in practice is generally confined to: keeping the lamps clean; renewing dud bulbs; topping-up the battery regularly; taking occasional specific-gravity readings; periodically inspecting the dynamo brushes and commutator (particularly important on 1945–51 models, but not applicable to any 1958–65 models); the keeping of all connexions clean and tight; and the prevention or repair of frayed leads by taping where necessary.

ILLUMINATION

The Switch Positions. The lighting switch (*see* Fig. 2) situated on top of 1955–65 headlamps causes the dynamo or alternator to charge in all three switch positions, which are as follows—
 "OFF"—No lights on.
 "L"—Headlamp pilot, rear lamp, and speedometer bulbs on.
 "H"—Headlamp main, rear lamp, and speedometer bulbs on.

Headlamp Alignment. Incorrect headlamp alignment gives reduced road illumination and liability to dazzle other road users.
 Many garages have a Lucas "Beamsetter," and advantage can be taken of one of these devices. To adjust the headlamp yourself, place your motorcycle so that it faces a light-coloured wall at a distance of about 25 feet. Switch on the main driving light and take vertical measurements from the centre of the headlamp and from the centre of the illuminated circle on the wall to the ground. Both measurements should be the same. If not, loosen the two fixing bolts securing the headlamp body and tilt the headlamp until the centre of the beam is truly parallel with the ground. Then retighten the two fixing bolts securely.

The 1955–7 Headlamps. As may be seen in Fig. 8, two smart torpedo-shaped pilot lamps are secured to the front-fork lamp supports by tubular bolts, through each of which a lead passes to the adjacent pilot lamp. The ammeter and lighting switch are mounted, one behind the other, on a panel on top of the headlamp, as shown.
 On all 1955–7 headlamps, to obtain access to the double filament "pre-focus" main bulb, remove the lamp front (with light-unit assembly)

as follows. Loosen the screw on top of the headlamp body, withdraw the rim outward from the top, and as the lamp front emerges raise it a little to free the lower tag from the shell of the headlamp. To get at the bulb in each streamlined pilot bulb, remove the screw at the rear and gently pull forward on the glass rim.

The 1958–65 Lucas Headlamp. Details of the Lucas type of headlamp fitted to 1958–65 A.J.S. machines are shown in Fig. 9. The light-unit

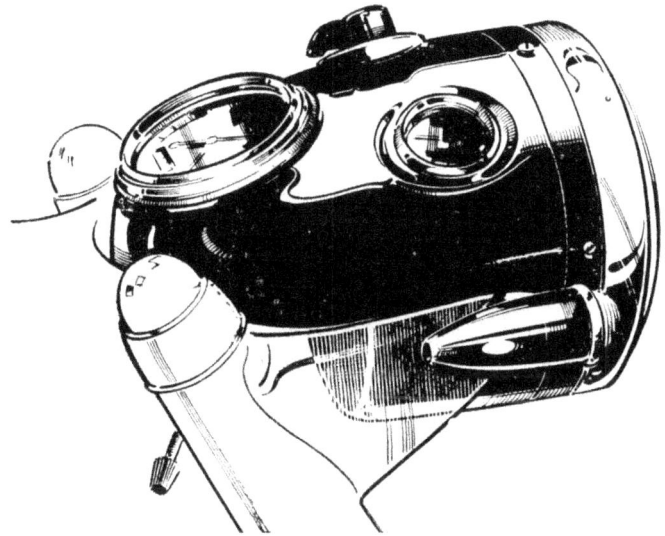

FIG. 8. LUCAS "PRE-FOCUS" HEADLAMP HOUSING AMMETER, LIGHTING SWITCH, AND SPEEDOMETER (1955–7)
(*By courtesy of "Motor Cycling"*)

assembly is shown removed from the headlamp body. On top of the headlamp body are mounted, as shown in Fig. 8, the Smith speedometer, the ammeter and the lighting switch. The three lighting switch positions are as described on page 20. On 1958–60 models with an alternator and rectifier instead of a magneto an ignition key is located in the centre of the lighting switch on 1958–60 models, or a separate ignition switch is provided (1961–5 models).

A "pre-focus" main bulb fits into a bulb holder at the rear of the reflector and is secured by a bayonet fixing adapter to which the three lighting cables are attached. The pilot or parking bulb below the main bulb is a push fit into the rear of the reflector.

To remove the lamp front (i.e. the light-unit assembly) to get access to the main and pilot bulbs, release the screw securing the lamp rim with one hand and support the light unit with the other. Then withdraw the light-unit assembly. Main bulb removal and fitting are effected as described below. To replace the light-unit assembly, engage the bottom tag on the lamp rim with the small slit in the lamp shield and gently press the top of the rim back into the lamp shell. Afterwards retighten the retaining screw on the top of the lamp body.

Separating Light Unit from Rim. On all Lucas 1955-65 type headlamps, the front glass and reflector are made as one assembly (the "light unit")

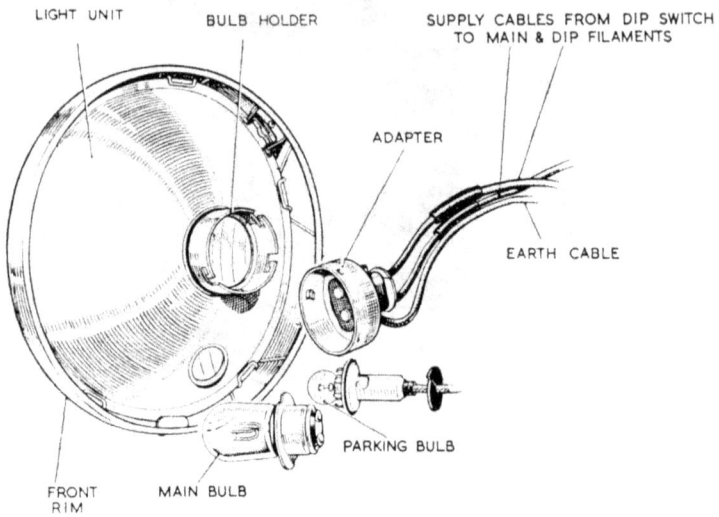

FIG. 9. LIGHT UNIT WITHDRAWN FROM LUCUS "PRE-FOCUS" HEADLAMP BODY (1958 ONWARDS)

and cannot be separated. The light unit, however, can be removed from the chromium-plated rim by disengaging the spring clips from the turned-up inner edge of the rim by pressing them with the blade of a screw-driver, working away from the edge.

To fit the light-unit assembly to the rim, lay the unit in the rim so that the location block on the unit engages the forked bracket on the rim, and then spring home the spring clips. See that they are spaced at equal distances around the rim.

Headlamp Bulb Renewal. Fit *genuine* Lucas bulbs if occasion arises to renew them, and do not defer renewal until actual bulb failure occurs.

When fitting a "pre-focus" bulb (*see* Fig. 9) turn the back shell anti-clockwise and withdraw it. You can then remove the bulb from the holder in the back of the reflector. Insert the correct Lucas-type bulb

THE LIGHTING SYSTEM

replacement in the bulb holder with its locating flange positioned, engage the projections on the inside of the adapter with the slots in the bulb holder, press on, and secure by turning clockwise.

Correct Bulb Renewals. The 1955–65 headlamps ("pre-focus" type) require a No. 312 (30/24-watt) Lucas double-filament main bulb which has a broad locating flange on the cap. An alternative bulb to the 6-volt No. 312 is the No. 373 (6-volt, 30/24-watt) Lucas double-filament bulb. Both bulbs are suitable for "pre-focus" lamps with block lens light units, but the No. 373 bulb has a left-hand dip and is now recommended by the manufacturers for use in Great Britain. On continental models fit a Lucas No. 403 (6-volt, 35/35-watt) double-filament bulb which has a vertical dip. All 1955–64 headlamps require a No. 988 pilot bulb. 1955 and later Lucas stop-tail lamps require a 6-volt, 18/6-watt, No. 384 double-filament bulb. The correct speedometer bulb is a 6-volt, 1·8-watt No. 53205 M.C.C.

The Ammeter. 1955–65 models have the ammeter and lighting switch built into the Lucas headlamp as shown in Fig. 8. It indicates the amount of current flowing into or from the battery. If no charge is shown with the engine running and the lamps switched off, obviously the dynamo or the alternator is for some reason not charging the battery. Do not meddle with the ammeter. If its needle sticks or "flutters," take the motor-cycle to the nearest Lucas service depot.

Cleaning Lucas Lamps. Being situated high up, a headlamp seldom becomes dirty, but keep the glass clean. Polish the enamelled surface of the headlamp body with a good wax polish and a soft duster. The chromium plated rim should be cleaned with a damp chamois leather and afterwards polished with a soft duster. Note that on 1955 and later "sealed beam" Lucas headlamps (with Lucas light unit) the reflector cannot be detached for cleaning.

Stop-tail Lamps. 1955 and later A.J.S. machines have Lucas stop-tail lamps of type 564. The lamp has a double-filament 6-volt, 6/18-watt bulb; the 6-watt filament serves as the normal rear light and the 18-watt filament is illuminated only when the rear-brake pedal is depressed. To obtain access to the bulb it is only necessary to remove two screws and withdraw the thermo-plastic cover. To prevent incorrect fitting of the No. 384 bulb, its securing pins are offset. The bulb has a small bayonet cap.

MAINTENANCE OF BATTERY

Neglect of the battery quickly brings trouble, and correct attention in regard to its maintenance is *vitally* important. Upon it depends the lamps and horn.

Topping-up the Battery. Examine the acid level about every three weeks, and even more frequently in tropical climates. Unscrew the battery clamping screw and remove the battery after first disconnecting the battery positive and negative leads. On 1956–65 models the Lucas battery is housed in a front compartment of the tool box as shown in Fig. 11. The battery must always be inserted with the negative terminal on the right-hand side of the battery compartment.

To remove the battery on 1956 models, first release the rubber strap by grasping the loop attached to its lower end; pull downwards until the

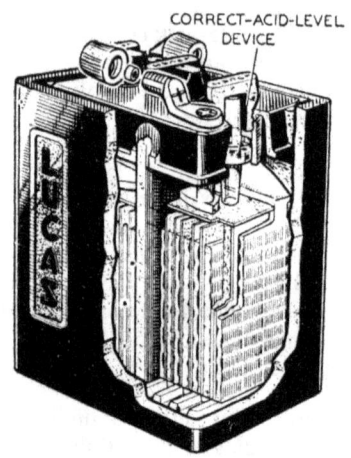

FIG. 10. KEEP THE ELECTROLYTE LEVEL WITH THE TOPS OF THE PLATE SEPARATORS (SEE ALSO FIG. 11)

The battery shown is the Lucas PU7E/11 or PUZ7E with correct-acid-level device, fitted to many 1956–65 models. The PU7E/9 battery fitted to 1955 models is similar except for modified terminals and the omission of external cell connectors.

strap and loop are freed from the retaining clip at the platform base, and permit the rubber strap to slacken. Then lift the battery out.

To remove the battery on 1957–65 models, grasp the rubber strap with the fingers between the battery case and rubber strap. Push the strap downwards until it is possible to free the metal toggle from the strap retaining-clip, then carefully take the battery out.

Take off the battery lid and remove the three vent plugs. Inspect the hole in each vent plug and make certain that it is not obstructed. A choked vent plug hole will result in an increase of pressure in the cell owing to "gassing," and this may cause trouble. Wipe the top of the battery clean with a rag and verify that the washer (where fitted) beneath each vent plug, to prevent leakage, is in position. After wiping the top of the battery, either destroy the rag or wash it thoroughly, using several changes of water. See that a supply of clean distilled water is to hand. Topping-up is necessary because the distilled water, unlike the acid, is gradually lost through evaporation.

Be careful not to hold a naked light near the vents. If the level is below the tops of the separators, add *distilled* water as required to bring the level correct. This should be done just *before* a charge run, as the agitation due to running and the gassing will thoroughly mix the solution. Acid

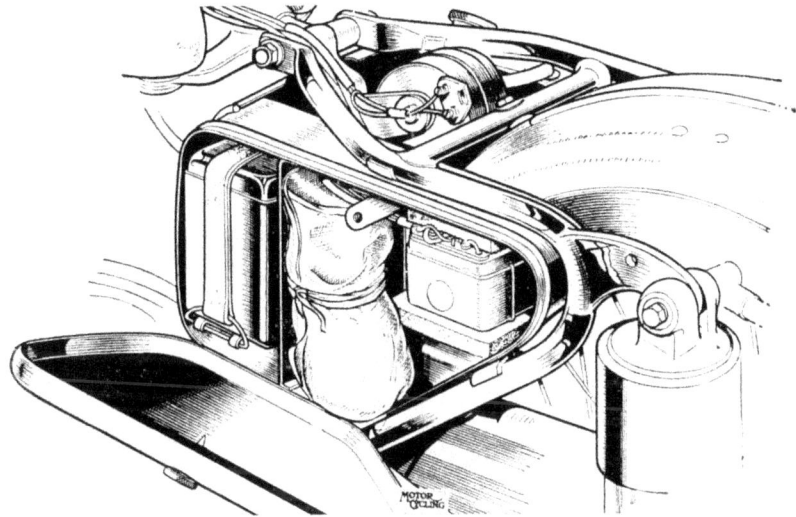

Fig. 11. A 1956–65 Refinement—Neat Enclosure of the Battery in the Tool Box

The compensated-voltage-control unit is, of course, omitted on 1958-65 models with coil ignition. The battery must be fitted with the negative terminal on the right-hand side. Top-up early Lucas batteries with no acid-level device with a Lucas battery filler so that the electrolyte is level with the tops of the separators. The more recent Lucas battery is the Lucas MLZ9E type. Top-up this type (not with a Lucas battery filler) so that the electrolyte reaches the level of the coloured line marked "maximum acid level" on its plastic case.
(*By courtesy of "Motor Cycling"*)

must not be added to the electrolyte unless the solution has been spilled. If the solution has been spilled by accident, add diluted sulphuric acid of specific gravity equal to that in the cells.

On A.J.S. machines with the PU7E/9 or PU7E/11 battery, pour distilled water round the flange (not the tube) of the acid-level device (*see* Fig. 10) until it ceases to drain into the cell. Then lift the tube slightly to enable the small amount of water in the flange to drain into the cell. The electrolyte level should then be correct. Inspect to make certain.

If the battery needs to be topped-up very often, it is possible that the

C.V.C. unit (1955-7) needs to be adjusted; if one cell requires more frequent topping-up than the others, probably the battery case or container is cracked, and battery renewal is called for.

Checking Specific Gravity. Very occasionally, hydrometer readings (specific-gravity values) should be taken of the solution in each of the cells. The method of doing this is shown in Fig. 12. The Lucas hydrometer

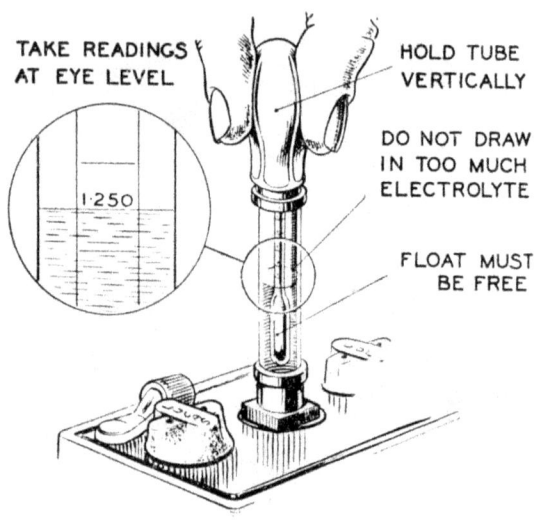

Fig. 12. Lucas Hydrometer being used to Check Specific Gravity of Battery Electrolyte

contains a graduated float which indicates the specific gravity of the battery cell from which a sample of electrolyte is taken.

After a sample has been taken and checked, it must, of course, be returned to the cell. The taking of S.G. readings with a hydrometer is the most efficient way of ascertaining the state of charge of the battery. The S.G. readings should be approximately the *same for all three cells*. Should the reading for one cell differ substantially from the readings for the others, probably some acid has been spilled or has leaked from the cell concerned. There is also a possibility of a short circuit between the battery plates. In the latter case it will be necessary to return the battery to a Lucas service depot for attention.

Under no circumstances must the battery be permitted to remain in a discharged condition for long, or serious deterioration will occur. After checking the S.G. readings and topping-up the cells, wipe the top of the battery and remove any spilled electrolyte or water; replace the three vent

THE LIGHTING SYSTEM

plugs and the battery lid. Then fit and tighten the battery clamping screw, or secure with the rubber strap (1956-65 models).

Battery Connexions. Always keep the battery connexions clean, free from corrosion, and tight, otherwise the ammeter readings will *not* indicate the true state of charge of the battery and proper battery charging may not occur.

Correct Readings. With Lucas batteries fitted to A.J.S. machines, the specific gravity readings at an acid temperature of approximately 60°F. should be: 1·270-1·290, battery fully charged; about 1·190-1·210 battery half discharged; 1·110-1·150 battery fully discharged. If the temperature exceeds 60°F., add 0·002 to the hydrometer reading for each 5 degrees rise in temperature above 60°F. Similarly if the temperature is below 60°F., deduct 0·002 for each 5 degrees decrease in temperature.

Never leave the battery in a discharged state for any appreciable period. A low state of charge is often caused through parking the machine for long periods with the lighting switch in the "L" position, unaccompanied by much daylight running. The remedy is, of course, to undertake more daylight running and to keep the switch in the "OFF" position as much as possible until the battery regains its normal state of charge. If overcharging occurs, have the setting of the compensated-voltage-control unit checked in the case of 1955-7 models.

MAINTENANCE OF DYNAMO (1955-7)

It is not necessary to take any special precautions when merely inspecting the commutator, but on making adjustments to the wiring circuit, it is essential to take steps to prevent accidental "shorting." Disconnect the lead from the lighting switch at the battery *negative* terminal. Push back the rubber shield and then unscrew the cable connector (where fitted). When doing this be sure that the cable does not make contact with any metal part of the frame, otherwise a "fat" spark will indicate that the battery *was* well charged! When reconnecting the lead, pull the rubber shield well over the connector.

General Overhaul. It is a good plan every 10,000-15,000 miles to entrust the dynamo to a Lucas service depot for dismantling, cleaning, servicing, and lubrication. Lubrication is referred to on page 49.

The Commutator and Brushgear. The Lucas E3AR and E3LM dynamos will run satisfactorily for thousands of miles without attention other than occasional inspection of the commutator and brushgear. It is advisable about every 5,000-6,000 miles, to remove the metal cover-band from the dynamo and make a careful inspection.

The Brushes. The brushes must make good electrical contact with the commutator. They must be absolutely clean and able to move freely in their box-type holders, on holding back the retaining springs and gently pulling the leads and then releasing them. There must also be perfect contact between both the brushes and the copper segments of the commutator; the brush faces in contact with the segments should be uniformly polished. Clean the brushes with a petrol-moistened cloth after removing them. To do this, pull back each brush-retaining spring (*see* Fig. 13) and remove the brush by pulling on its lead, being careful to see that the brush pressure-spring is clear of the brush holder.

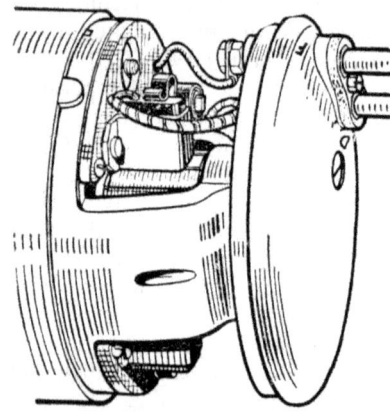

Fig. 13. Commutator End of the Lucas E3LM Dynamo with Cover Band Removed

Examine the carbon brushes for wear and unevenness, and true them up if necessary. Generally it is best to renew the brushes *before* serious wear develops, as this prevents sparking, which causes blackening of the commutator and an unsteady charging current. Always replace brushes in their original positions.

If Lucas brushes become so badly worn that it is necessary to remove them, this can easily be done as follows: Release the eyelet on the brush lead by unscrewing the hexagonal nut or screw at the terminal; then, holding back the spring lever out of the way, withdraw the brush from its holder. Renew with genuine Lucas brushes.

The brush springs should be inspected occasionally to see that they have sufficient tension to keep the brushes firmly pressed against the commutator when the dynamo is running. It is particularly necessary to keep this in mind when the brushes have been in use a long time and are very much worn down.

It is unwise to insert brushes of a grade other than that supplied with the dynamo, or to change the tension springs. The arrangement provided has been made only after many years' experience and will be found to give the best results and the longest life. It is really best, when the brushes become so worn that they no longer bed down on the commutator, or their flexible leads are exposed on their running faces, to have new brushes fitted at a Lucas service depot, as this ensures the brushes being properly "bedded."

The Commutator Surface. The surface of the commutator segments should be kept clean and free from oil or brush dust, etc. Should any

THE LIGHTING SYSTEM 29

grease or oil work its way on to the commutator through over-lubrication, it will not only cause sparking, but, in addition, carbon and copper dust will collect in the grooves between the commutator segments.

The best way to clean the commutator is, without disconnecting any leads, to remove from its box-holder one of the main brushes and, inserting a fine dry duster, hold it, with a suitably-shaped piece of wood, against the commutator surface, causing the armature to be rotated by the kick-starter.* If the commutator is very dirty, first moisten the cloth with petrol. The segments should be *dark bronze* and highly polished.

To Adjust Dynamo Chain. The tension of the dynamo chain which lies behind the primary chain (*see* Fig. 55) should be checked occasionally, after removing the oil-bath chain case inspection cap (*see* page 52). Chain whip with the chain in its tightest position, mid-way between the sprockets, should be approximately $\frac{1}{4}$ in.

To make an eccentric adjustment for chain tension, first slacken the strap bolt clamping the dynamo in its housing. Now rotate the dynamo *anti-clockwise* (with the fingers, 1955–7 models) until chain tension is felt to be correct on passing a finger through the inspection-cap opening. Be careful not to confuse the primary chain with the dynamo chain which lies *behind* the former (*see* Fig. 55). Afterwards retighten the strap bolt and again check the tension of the dynamo chain. If found to be correct, replace the inspection cap on the oil-bath chain case (*see* page 52).

Compensated Voltage Control. All 1955–7 A.J.S. motor-cycles incorporate compensated voltage control. The C.V.C. unit consists of a cut-out and voltage-regulator unit in a box beneath the saddle, beside the battery carrier, or (1956–7) in the tool box. It is connected between the dynamo and battery and ensures that the battery is automatically charged the right amount by varying the dynamo output according to the state of charge of the battery and the load imposed on it.

Current is prevented from flowing back from the battery to the dynamo at low r.p.m. by means of the cut-out which opens. As soon as the r.p.m. rise high enough to enable the dynamo to charge the battery, the cut-out closes and completes the circuit.

In all three lighting-switch positions (*see* page 20) the dynamo gives a controlled output and thus relieves you of responsibility in regard to charging. The regulator begins to operate when the dynamo voltage reaches about 7·3 volt. During daylight running with the battery well charged and the switch in the "OFF" position, the dynamo gives only a trickle charge, and the ammeter reading is unlikely to exceed 1–2 amp. There is no danger of over-charging.

The regulator provides for an increase of dynamo output as soon as the

---

* Slow rotation is assisted by removing the sparking plug.

lamps are switched on. The effect of switching the lamps on after a long run with the battery voltage high is often to cause a temporary discharge reading at the ammeter, but fairly soon the voltage falls and the regulator responds, thereby causing the output of the dynamo to balance the load of the lamps.

When the battery is in a discharged state, the regulator increases the dynamo output and restores the battery to its normal state of charge in the shortest possible time.

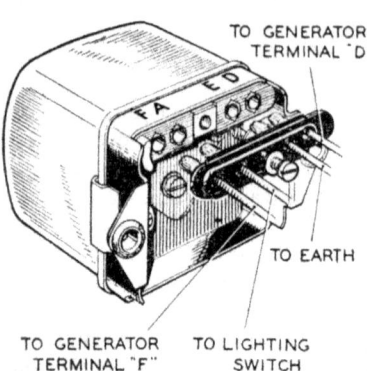

FIG. 14. LUCAS CUT-OUT AND REGULATOR UNIT SHOWING THE CONNEXIONS

Do Not Tamper with C.V.C. Unit. The unit is sealed by the makers, as it should not need adjustment once it is correctly set. If, however, the battery (in good condition) is persistently under-charged or over-charged, suspect the C.V.C. unit setting and have it checked, preferably at a Lucas service depot. Note that the C.V.C. unit is retained by self-locking nuts, except on 1956-7 models where it is retained in a sponge-rubber holder in a partition at the rear top corner of the tool box (see Fig. 11). To remove the C.V.C. unit on a 1956-7 model, grasp it between the fingers and thumb of one hand, and gently and firmly pull it away from the sponge-rubber holder.

As may be seen in Fig. 14, the four terminals of the C.V.C. unit are clearly marked by the letters *F.A.E.D.* Leads from the *F* and *D* terminals are attached to similarly marked terminals on the dynamo. The terminal marked *A* is connected to one of the ammeter terminals, and the terminal marked *E* is earthed.

To Remove the Dynamo (1955-7). On machines with the magneto positioned in front of the engine, dynamo removal is very straightforward and no retiming of the magneto is necessary.

First remove the near-side footrest arm. Lay a drip-tray beneath the oil-bath chain case to receive the oil, and remove the outer portion of the oil-bath chain case (*see* page 109). Next remove the spring circlip, the locking plate, and the nut securing the dynamo sprocket, and with a suitable tool withdraw the sprocket. While slackening the sprocket-retaining nut, hold the sprocket with the appropriate spanner (Part No. 017254). This prevents any bending stress being imposed on the spindle of the dynamo.

Disconnect the dynamo leads and slacken the dynamo clamping-bolt

THE LIGHTING SYSTEM 31

fully. Now twist the dynamo by hand until the locating strip on its body aligns with the key-way cut-away in the rear engine plate housing the dynamo. Then withdraw the dynamo, tilting it upwards so as to clear the gearbox.

To Replace the Dynamo (1955–7). Observe the removal instructions in reverse. Be careful to locate the dynamo-sprocket key accurately when fitting the dynamo sprocket. Also check that the dynamo chain is correctly tensioned (see page 29), and follow the instructions given (page 109) for replacing the outer half of the oil-bath chain case. Before fitting this outer half, make sure that the dynamo sprocket securing-nut is firmly tightened prior to the fitting of the locking plate and the retaining circlip.

Removal of Dynamo Chain (1955–7 Models). First remove the outer half of the oil-bath chain case (see page 109). Next remove the nut retaining the engine sprocket. This is facilitated by engaging top gear and applying the rear brake. Withdraw the shock-absorber spring, cupped washer, and cam. Now remove the primary chain to obtain access to the dynamo chain. Remove the spring circlip from the nut retaining the sprocket on the dynamo armature. Also detach the locking washer or plate which surrounds the nut. With the appropriate spanner (Part No. 017254) applied to the two flats on the back of the dynamo sprocket, hold the sprocket and unscrew the dynamo-sprocket retaining nut. With a suitable extractor tool release the dynamo sprocket from the armature. Now remove in one operation the dynamo sprocket, "endless" dynamo chain, and the engine-sprocket assembly.

Replacing Dynamo Sprocket, Chain, and Engine Sprocket (1955–7). Check that the key for the dynamo sprocket is in position on the armature location. Also verify that the spacing collar (between the crankcase ball bearing and the back of the engine sprocket) is replaced on the engine driving-side mainshaft. Next engage the dynamo driving chain with the teeth of the dynamo driving sprocket (the smaller sprocket of the engine-sprocket assembly) and the sprocket which fits on the dynamo armature. In one simultaneous operation replace the two sprockets (and chain) on the engine mainshaft and dynamo armature. Then replace the plain washer and sprocket retaining nut on the dynamo armature. Tighten the nut finger-tight only.

While preventing the dynamo armature from turning by applying the appropriate spanner (Part No. 017254) to the flats on the back of the sprocket, tighten the dynamo-sprocket retaining nut firmly. Replace the locking washer or plate for the retaining nut, also the retaining circlip. Make sure that the latter beds down properly in the nut groove. Finally replace the cam of the engine shaft shock-absorber, the spring, cap washer, and retaining nut. Also replace the primary chain and check its tension (*see* page 99). The outer half of the oil-bath chain case can now be replaced (*see* page 109).

THE ALTERNATOR AND RECTIFIER (1958–65)

The Lucas RM15 and RM19 Alternator. The alternator on 1958–65 models comprises a spigot-mounted 6-coil laminated stator bolted to the oil-bath chain case cover (*see* Fig. 56), with a rotor carried on and driven by an

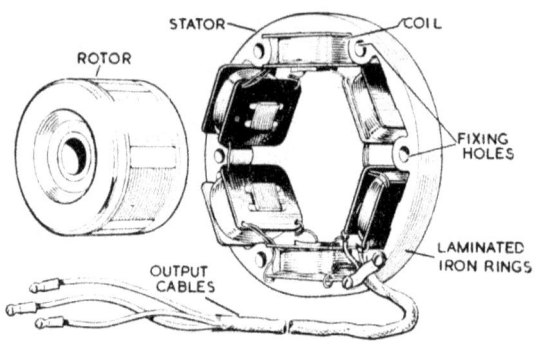

FIG. 15. SHOWING DETAILS OF LUCAS RM15 AND RM19 ALTERNATOR
Applicable to 1958–65 A.J.S. Models 16, 18. For position on machine, *see* Fig. 56.

extension of the crankshaft. The aluminium rotor has a hexagonal steel core, each face of which carries a permanent magnet keyed to a laminated pole tip.

Because, unlike the Lucas dynamos fitted to 1955–7 models, the alternator and stator have no rotating windings, commutator, brushgear, bearings, or oil seals, no maintenance whatever is called for other than to see that the three snap-connexions in the output cables (*see* Fig. 15) are tight and clean, and the leads unfrayed. The snap-connexions, by the way, are located behind the frame cover which is secured by two knurled screws.

Should it be necessary for any reason to withdraw the rotor, there is no need to fit keepers to the rotor poles. After removing a rotor wipe off any metal swarf which may have collected on the pole tips. Place the rotor in a clean place.

To Remove A.C. Rotor. The rotor is keyed to the engine shaft. If removal is required for some reason, first remove the outer half of the oil-bath chain case (*see* page 110). Next engage top gear and apply pressure to the rear brake pedal. Then unscrew the lock-nut and the nut securing the rotor. Withdraw the washer and pull off the rotor.

THE LIGHTING SYSTEM

The Alternator Output Control. While riding normally with the ignition switch in the "ON" position the rate of output depends on the position of the lighting switch, electrical energy passing through the battery from the alternator in the form of rectified alternating current.

When the lighting switch is turned to the "OFF" position the alternator output supplies the ignition coil and trickle-charges the battery. When the lighting switch is turned to the "L" or "H" position the alternator output is automatically increased to meet the extra load.

Altering the Alternator Connexions. In the event of the battery becoming discharged it is possible to effect a temporary boost by altering the alternator connexions behind the frame plate after removing the two knurled screws and removing the plate. Alter the connexions in the following manner.

On 1958–60 models disconnect the green and yellow and dark green connectors. Reconnect the dark green cable connector to the green and yellow cable connector. Do not interfere with the light green cable.

On 1961–5 models disconnect the green and yellow and green and black connectors. Reconnect the green and black to the green and yellow. Do not interfere with the green and white cable.

Note that prolonged use of the machine with the alternator connexions altered is not recommended and will *harm the battery*.

The Lucas Rectifier. The Lucas rectifier is housed on the tool box below the dualseat. The rectifier consists of four plates (coated on one side with selenium) and functions like a non-return valve, permitting current to pass in one direction only. The alternating current from the alternator is thus converted to unidirectional (d.c.) current for charging the battery. The rectifier needs no maintenance other than to keep the connexions clean and tight, and to check periodically that the nut securing the rectifier to the frame of the motor-cycle is tight. *Do not in any circumstances loosen the nut which clamps the rectifier plates together.* The nut is most carefully adjusted during manufacture to give optimum performance.

The Rectifier Connexions. Should the leads be disconnected from the rectifier it is vital to see that they are reconnected correctly. Fig. 16 shows how the coloured cables should be connected to the rectifier. Never alter this arrangement.

THE HORN

Careful adjustment of the Lucas horn is made at the works, and subsequent adjustment is rarely called for. Normally the horn should give long service without any attention whatever. The vibrating parts do, however, gradually wear and, after very considerable usage, some roughness and loss of tone may develop. This necessitates an examination being made at a Lucas service depot.

If Horn Fails Completely or Partially. Do not immediately infer that the horn has broken down or needs adjustment. Possible causes of the

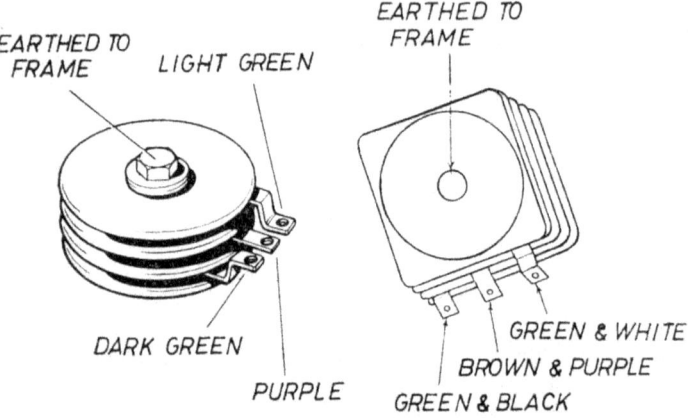

Fig. 16. The Lucas Rectifier showing Connexions
The rectifier shown on the left is fitted to 1958–60 models. That on the right is fitted to 1961–3 models.

trouble are: a loose fixing bolt; vibration of some adjacent part; a discharged battery; a loose connexion; a short circuit in the wiring; or a defective push-switch. The last-mentioned may be occasioned through poor electrical contact with the handlebars.

THE WIRING SYSTEM

No Fuse. There is no fuse incorporated in the wiring circuit, which is purposely simplified, and capable of being understood by those with elementary electrical knowledge. If care is taken to keep the various wires correctly connected, and to maintain the connexions clean and firm, there is no risk of an excessive current damaging any of the equipment or wiring.

Inspect the Wiring Occasionally. It is advisable occasionally to make a careful inspection of the wiring, especially of the wires from the battery, the leads from the dynamo to the C.V.C. unit, or the alternator output cables (1958–65). See that the insulation is sound and not chafed and

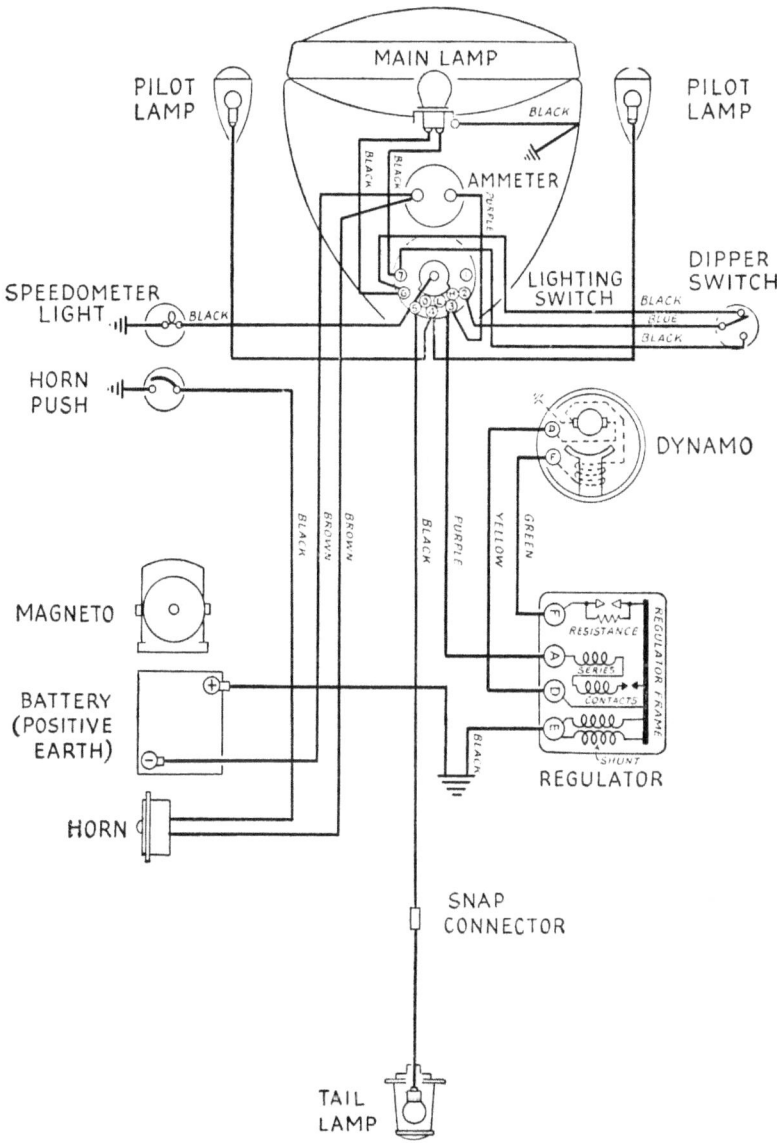

Fig. 17. Wiring Diagram for all 1955-7 Models (Positive Earth)

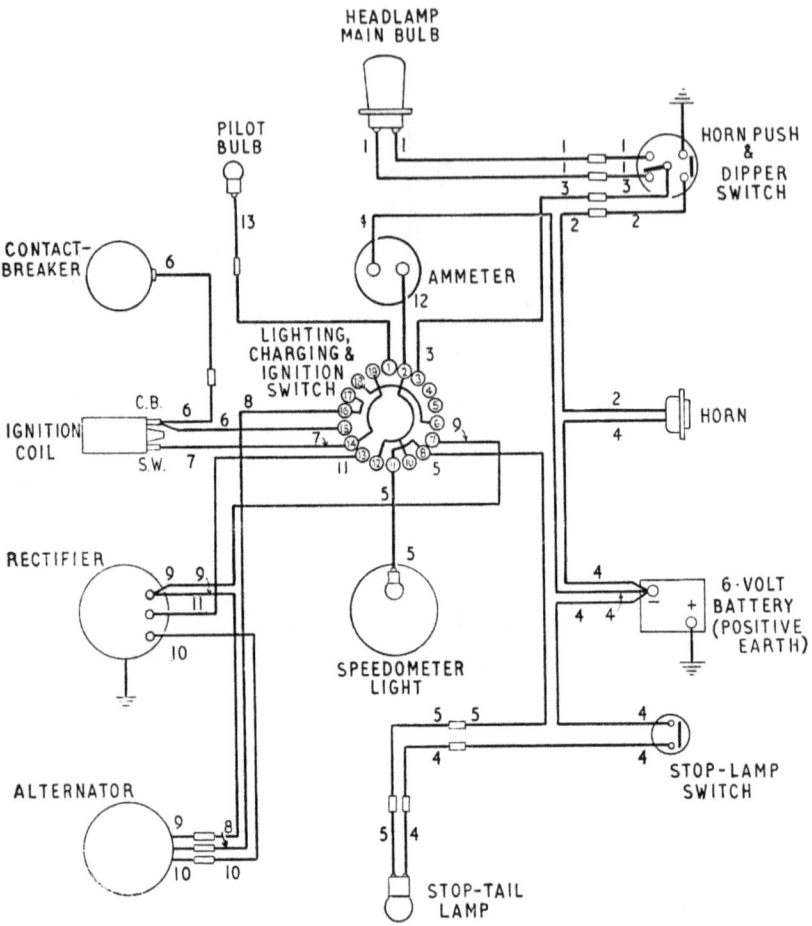

FIG. 18. WIRING DIAGRAM FOR ALL 1958–9 MODELS (POSITIVE EARTH)

KEY TO SLEEVE COLOURS

1. Black.
2. Brown and black.
3. Blue.
4. Brown and blue.
5. Brown and green.
6. Black and white.
7. White.
8. Green and yellow.
9. Dark green.
10. Light green.
11. Purple.
12. Brown and white.
13. Red.

THE LIGHTING SYSTEM

that all connexions are clean and tight. Should a dynamo fail to charge, this may be due to dynamo trouble, a faulty lead, or a faulty C.V.C. unit. Tape up any loose or frayed leads.

As may be seen in Figs. 17-19, the ends of leads can be identified for connexion purposes by means of their coloured sleeves. This greatly

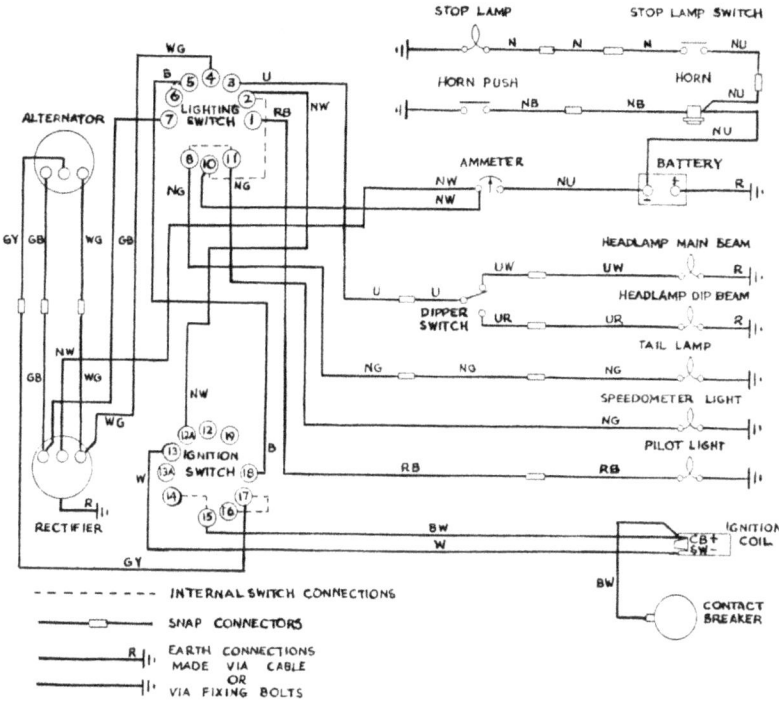

FIG. 19. WIRING DIAGRAM FOR ALL 1960-5 MODELS (POSITIVE EARTH)

KEY TO SLEEVE COLOURS

B. Black.
G. Green.
L. Light.
N. Brown.
P. Purple.
R. Red.
U. Blue.
W. White.
Y. Yellow.

facilitates reconnecting the wiring circuit in the event of the wires being disconnected from the various terminals.

The leads connected to the terminals marked D and F on a dynamo and C.V.C. unit must on no account be reversed. To prevent this being done, the screw in the dynamo terminal block is off-centre, and the screws securing the regulator clamping-plate are of different size.

An Important Precaution. It is extremely important to disconnect one of the battery leads (*see* page 27) if making any alterations to the wiring or removing the lighting switch from the Lucas headlamp. *On all* 1955-65 *models the battery positive terminal is earthed.* The earth connexion is connected to the dualseat lug tube. The dualseat must be removed to obtain access to it.

The Battery Lead Connexions. On all later (MLZ9E, PUZ7E type) Lucas batteries detachable lead-connectors are provided at the battery terminals. To make a lead connexion, unscrew the knurled terminal nut and withdraw the collet or cone-shaped insert. Note that the inserts for the two terminals are not interchangeable. After baring the lead end for about an inch, thread the bared end through the knurled nut and collet. Then insert the collet and cable into the terminal block after first bending the wire strands over the narrow end of the collet. Tighten the knurled nut firmly to secure the connexion.

CHAPTER IV

CORRECT LUBRICATION

THE A.J.S. design dept. have done their best to ensure that correct lubrication involves the minimum attention by the rider. This attention, however, is *absolutely vital* and is dealt with in detail in this chapter.

Neglect to lubricate the engine and machine properly causes excessive friction and heat, accompanied by undue wear of the contacting bearing

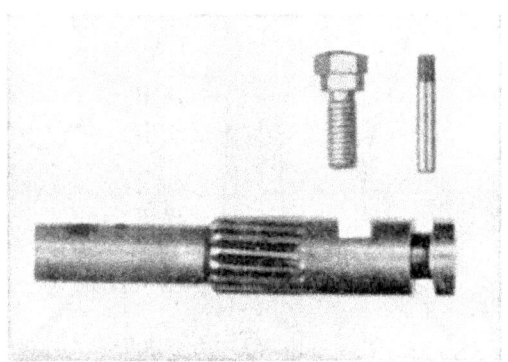

FIG. 20. THE "HEART" OF THE 1955–63 A.J.S. LUBRICATION SYSTEM

The oil pump is positioned on the engine as shown in Fig. 21. Above are shown the pump plunger, the guide screw, and the steel pin which fits inside the hollow guide screw with the relieved end (shown dark) *away from* the plunger. The plunger and the guide screw should not be disturbed during routine maintenance. 1964–5 models have a gear-type oil pump.

surfaces. Such neglect can rapidly spoil a good motor-cycle and cause heavy repair bills, besides reducing performance.

ENGINE LUBRICATION

The engine lubrication system on all A.J.S. O.H.V. models is of the full dry-sump (D.S.) type, where *all* oil in the engine and oil tank is kept in constant circulation while the engine is running. Its functioning is entirely automatic, but a little regular attention is *essential*.

The 1955–63 Oil Pump. The oil pump in the crankcase has a horizontal-type steel plunger (Fig. 20) which combines rotary motion with reciprocating movement. Rotary motion is imparted to the plunger by a worm on

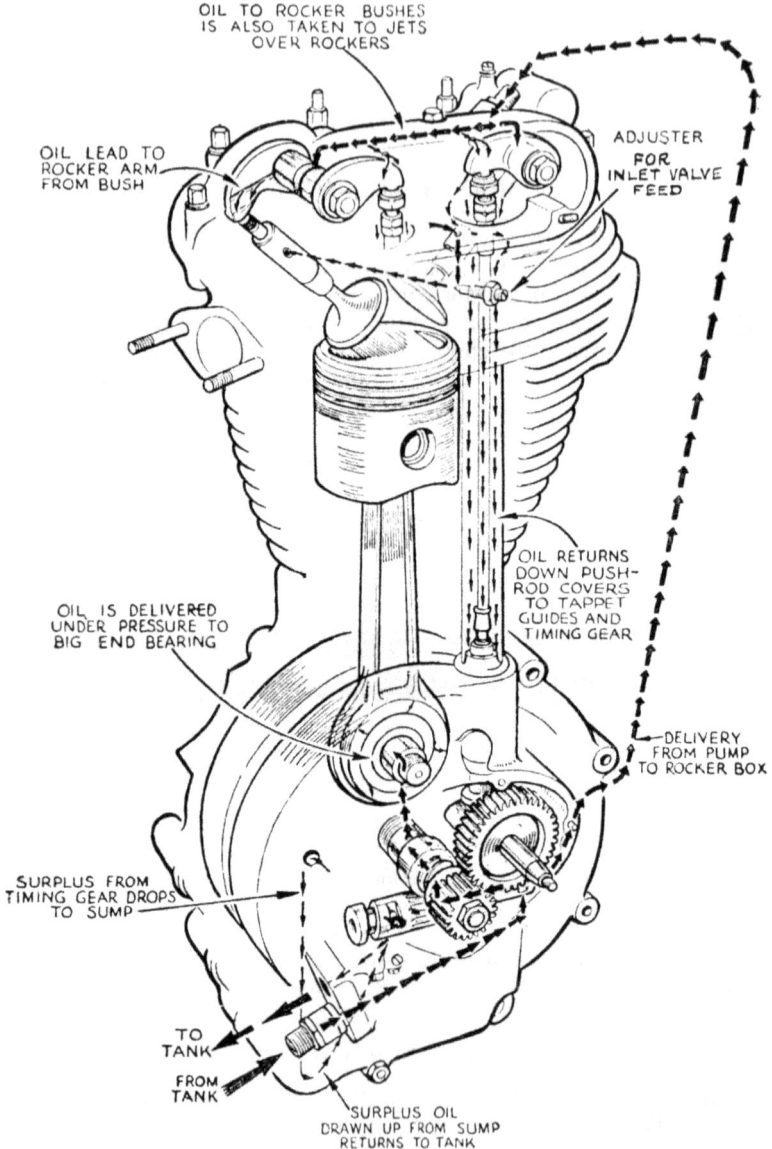

FIG. 21. OIL CIRCULATION DIAGRAM (1956–63 ENGINES)

This diagram also applies to 1955 engines except for the following: 1955 engines have a circular channel in the cylinder base feeding holes in the cylinder wall; 1964–5 engines have a gear-type oil pump driven by a worm on the timing-side mainshaft. A by-pass from the main oil feed taken from the timing cover positively lubricates the overhead rockers.

the timing-side engine mainshaft. The reciprocating motion is obtained by the hardened pin in the hollow guide screw (*see* Fig. 20) engaging the profiled cam-groove cut on the (larger) scavenge end of the plunger.

The profiled cam-groove is designed so that the opening and closing of the two main ports, and a small auxiliary port, are synchronized with the pumping impulses obtained by plunger reciprocation. The scavenge (rear) end of the plunger (which is totally enclosed in its housing by two end-caps) has a greater capacity than the delivery end, and in consequence

FIG. 22. THE "HEART" OF THE 1964–5 A.J.S. LUBRICATION SYSTEM
A gear-type oil pump similar to that shown above is used instead of the rotating and reciprocating plunger type shown in Fig. 20. The later pump delivers oil at a higher pressure than the earlier pump.

it keeps the crankcase sump in a "dry" state, all oil being returned to the tank for further circulation.

The 1964–5 Oil Pump. A gear-type oil pump (*see* Fig. 22) is provided on 1964–5 models. The gears on the return side of the pump are twice as wide as those on the feed side and therefore, having twice the pumping capacity, effectively keep the crankcase "dry," all oil being returned to the oil tank for further circulation. The pump, which has no adjustment, is driven by the worm gear on the timing-side mainshaft. Its body is secured by two studs and nuts. A conical shaped heat-resisting rubber oil seal is attached to the pump body, where it abuts against a drilling in the timing cover.

How the Oil Circulates. Fig. 21 shows at a glance how the oil circulates in the A.J.S. engine with D.S. lubrication. The filtration of the oil in the tank (capacity: $4\frac{1}{2}$ pt., 1955; 5 pt., 1956; 4 pt., 1957–65) is shown in Figs. 23 and 24.

The delivery end of the plunger or gear pump feeds oil under pressure to the timing-side main bearing and connecting-rod big-end bearing through a passage cut in the timing-side mainshaft, flywheel, and crankpin. The piston and cylinder bore are lubricated by surplus oil splashed from the big-end bearing. Further provision for lubrication of the cylinder is included on 1955 engines. The oil pump forces oil through a passage (equipped with ball-valve control) in the crankcase to a circular channel in the cylinder base. The oil reaches the cylinder bore through a number of small holes drilled in the channel. Surplus oil automatically drains down into the sump of the crankcase.

The A.J.S. oil pump also feeds a secondary oil supply to the timing gear and rocker-box. The supply to the timing gear is fed through a passage in the timing-gear case. The oil collects in the timing-case until a pre-determined level is reached. As may be seen in Fig. 21, on 1955-63 engines an external pipe connected to the front of the oil-pump housing conveys the secondary oil-supply direct to the overhead rockers and push-rod ends.

The overhead inlet and exhaust-valve rockers inside the rocker-box are thoroughly lubricated by means of jets above them. In addition, oil is fed to the rocker bushes and (1955 onwards) each rocker arm. The surplus oil drains to and lubricates both valve guides. The oil supply to the guide for the inlet valve can be regulated by means of a needle-pointed screw adjuster. This oil-supply adjustment is the only one provided on the A.J.S. dry-sump lubrication system.

Surplus oil from the valve gear passes down the push-rod covers and the tappet guides and enters the timing case. Here all engine oil, beyond that needed to keep the level at the predetermined height, drains down into the sump of the crankcase. The large-capacity scavenge end of the oil pump sucks up the oil collected in the sump from various parts of the engine and pumps it back via the upper pipe into the oil tank for filtering and further circulation.

The whole of the oil in the tank and the engine is thus kept in constant circulation and the sump remains practically "dry." A crankcase pressure-release valve is incorporated in the driving-side mainshaft and the crankcase has a magnetic filter in the sump.

The Tank Filters. Clean every 5,000 miles. A cut-away view of the A.J.S. oil tank is shown in Figs. 23 and 24. As may be observed, a metal-gauze filter is incorporated in the delivery or feed-pipe union. It should be noted that the sole object of this filter is to trap any dirt, pieces of fluff, etc., which may get into the oil tank while it is being replenished.

The main filter (1955 models) is a detachable fabric-type. It comprises a long felt-element contained within an upright tubular wire cage. As may be noticed in Fig. 23, all the engine oil returned by the scavenge end of the pump has to percolate through the felt element and wire cage which are supported by a cylindrical housing inside the tank. Very thorough filtering results. On 1956-65 models a fabric-type filter with felt element is not fitted. Instead, a cylindrical filter of fine metal-gauze is secured in the tank end of the feed-pipe union.

Always purchase engine oil in sealed containers or replenish from

CORRECT LUBRICATION

branded cabinets. Specify clearly the brand and grade which you require, and refuse firmly but politely the "just as good" type.

Suitable Engine Oils. To ensure easy starting, maximum performance and minimum wear, the safest policy is to use one of the brands and grades officially recommended by Matchless Motor Cycles, Ltd. They recommend the use of one of the following engine oils—
  (a) Castrol "Grand Prix" (summer) or "XL" (winter).
  (b) Mobiloil "D" (summer) or "A" (winter).
  (c) Shell X-100 50 (summer) or X-100 30 (winter).

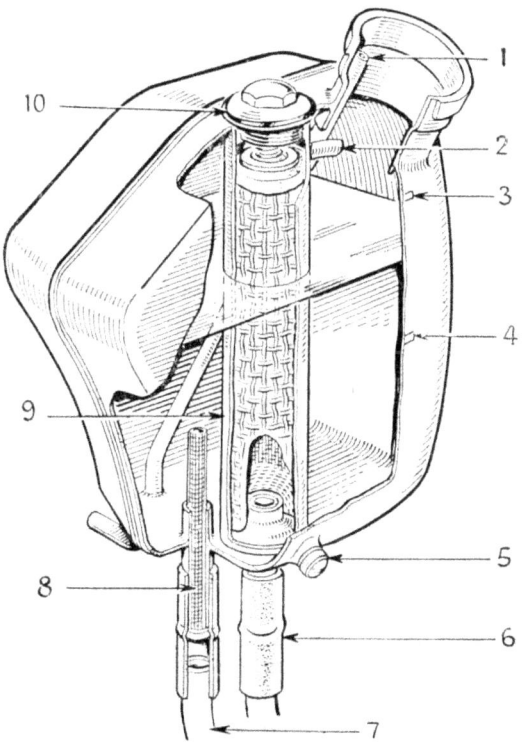

FIG. 23. CUT-AWAY VIEW OF OIL TANK SHOWING THE FILTERS, ETC. (1955 MODELS)

KEY TO FIG. 23

1. Vent pipe (to prevent air locks).
2. Oil-return pipe orifice.
3. Top-level mark.
4. Low-level mark.
5. Drain plug.
6. Oil-return pipe.
7. Oil-feed pipe.
8. Gauze filter.
9. Tube enclosing felt element.
10. Cap on main filter.

(d) B.P. Energol SAE 50 (summer) or B.P. Energol SAE 30 (winter).
(e) Essolube 50 (summer) or Essolube 30 (winter).

It should be noted that the above recommendations are not tabulated in any priority order. It is for the rider to choose which brand he prefers. All the five mentioned are thoroughly sound.

Oil Level in Tank. Remove the filler cap and inspect the level of oil prior to every ride. Always verify the level very carefully before a long

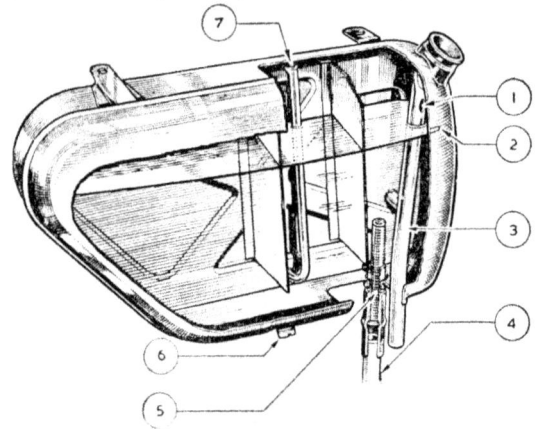

FIG. 24. CUT-AWAY VIEW OF OIL TANK ON 1956–65 MODELS

KEY TO FIG. 24

1. Oil-return pipe orifice.
2. Top-level mark.
3. Oil-return pipe.
4. Oil-feed pipe.
5. Gauze filter (metal).
6. Drain plug.
7. Air vent pipe.

run and top up with suitable engine oil (*see* previous paragraph) if necessary. Sufficient oil must be kept circulating to ensure correct lubrication of the engine and its proper cooling.

Never allow the oil level to fall below the low-level mark, otherwise the oil in circulation is apt to become hot, dirty, and diluted. As far as possible maintain the oil level at or near the top-level mark on the outside of the tank (1955–65), but do not allow the level to rise above this mark. This is important for the following reason.

On stopping the engine, no further pump action occurs, but the oil continues to drain into the sump from various parts of the engine. When the engine is subsequently started there is obviously surplus oil accumulated in the sump and this is immediately pumped back into the tank by the large-capacity scavenge side of the pump. The effect is to cause an excessive rise in the level of oil in the tank, and possibly oil leakage via the tank air-vent (provided to avoid air locks).

CORRECT LUBRICATION 45

Checking Oil Circulation. Verify the oil circulation before *every run*, immediately after starting up the engine from cold. Remove the oil tank filler-cap and observe the oil flow from the small spout (*see* Fig. 24) about 2 in. below the filler-cap orifice. If no oil can be seen emerging from the spout, raise the exhaust-valve lifter and stop the engine immediately.

The oil flow immediately after starting up the engine from cold should be *steady*. An erratic or weak flow is abnormal and requires investigation. After a brief period of warming up the engine, the surplus oil in the crank-case sump is disposed of, and thereafter the oil flow from the spout of the return pipe decreases somewhat and may become irregular. Some froth may be noticeable caused by the presence of air bubbles, but this is normal and can be disregarded, once the engine gets into its stride.

If you suddenly accelerate the engine and then close back the throttle, you may observe first a marked decline, or even cessation, of the oil flow and then a considerable increase in the flow.

No Pump Adjustment. The A.J.S. oil pump is capable of delivering the correct volume of oil to the engine at *all* throttle openings. Consequently there is no adjustment provided for the main oil supply. To ensure correct lubrication of the engine, however, it is essential on 1955–63 models to keep the two end-caps of the plunger housing quite airtight. Check the securing nuts periodically for tightness with a spanner. (*See also* page 47.)

Oil Supply to Inlet-valve Stem. The adjuster for the oil supply to the inlet-valve stem comprises a needle-pointed screw (Fig. 21) situated on the off-side of the cylinder head. If the engine is mechanically sound, the approximately correct setting of the adjuster screw is *one-sixth of a complete turn from the fully closed position*. Once the correct setting has been obtained, it should not be necessary to interfere with the adjustment.

The adjuster screw is secured by a lock-nut, which prevents accidental alteration of the adjustment. To *increase* or decrease the oil supply to the inlet-valve stem, the adjuster screw must be turned slightly *anti-clockwise* or clockwise respectively, after first loosening the lock-nut.

What symptoms indicate that an adjustment is called for? An excessive oil supply is denoted by blue smoke at the exhaust, high oil consumption, and a tendency for the sparking plug to oil up and become dirty. An insufficient oil supply is indicated by the inlet-valve stem developing a mouse-like squeak.

The Exhaust-valve Stem. No adjustment is provided for the oil supply to the exhaust-valve stem. The stem is automatically lubricated by oil fed through a channel drilled in the cylinder head. Surplus oil from the ex-haust-valve stem and from the stem of the inlet valve is by-passed back into the chamber responsible for lubricating the timing gears.

Changing the Oil. With a brand-new A.J.S. it is advisable to empty the oil tank and replenish it with fresh oil after covering 500 miles and again at 1,000 miles. After this, change the oil once every 5,000 miles. If a machine is only used for short runs, renew the oil every three months. Also clean the tank filter (two on 1955 models).

Before draining the oil tank, make sure that your A.J.S. is level, with both wheels on the ground or with the stand down. Then to drain the tank, place a suitable receptacle below the drain plug to catch the oil and unscrew the plug from the off-side edge of the tank. Be patient and allow all the oil to drain away.

Having drained the oil tank, also remove the drain plug from the bottom of the crankcase sump (on the off-side), and permit any accumulation of oil to drain off. There will not be a large amount, but it is desirable to remove what there is. A powerful magnetic filter is fitted to the crankcase drain-plug on 1956 and later models and it is important to see that the accumulation of any fine metallic particles is completely removed. Finally, make sure that both drain plugs are replaced and firmly tightened.

The Magnetic Crankcase Filter (1956–65). Forcibly wipe off with a greased rag all metal particles adhering to the magnetic filter (they adhere strongly). If you place the filter on the bench see that the magnet does not come into contact with large iron or steel objects, such as a vice, otherwise some loss of magnetism may occur. Also avoid placing the magnet close to iron or steel filings, which will be attracted to the magnetic filter and need removing.

The Tank Filters. Thorough and regular cleaning of the two filters in the oil tank (one, 1956–65) is most important and must never be overlooked. It is best to remove and clean the filter(s) after the engine oil is changed. Advice on removing the filters is given in subsequent paragraphs. As regards actual cleaning, this should be done thoroughly with petrol, but do not attempt to remove the felt element of a large cartridge-type filter from its tubular wire cage, and do not use a fluffy rag when cleaning a gauze filter. Allow to dry afterwards.

Inspect the cork washer fitted below the hexagon cap of a fabric filter (Fig. 23) and renew the washer if it is not in perfect condition. Also examine the felt element very carefully. Fit a new element if its ends are at all distorted or perforated.

It should be observed that a choked gauze filter can completely or partially starve the engine of oil, since it is secured to the feed-pipe union and all oil entering the engine has to pass through it.

If the felt element of a fabric filter is clogged up with impurities, excessive lubrication can occur owing to resistance offered to the returning oil causing a "build-up" of oil in the sump. Renew the filter element if its condition is poor.

CORRECT LUBRICATION 47

To Remove Felt Element (1955 Models). Unscrew and remove the hexagonal cap from the oil tank filler-orifice. Next withdraw the dished washer and the filter spring. After withdrawing the dished washer and filter spring, insert a finger in the exposed open end of the felt element and gently strain outward and forward (spring-frame models) to avoid fouling the dualseat. Be most careful not to kink the element when doing this.

The procedure for replacing the filter element is the reverse of that just described.

To Remove Gauze Filter (1955-64). Referring to Fig. 24, first drain the oil tank and then (1955-6) free the oil-feed pipe from the rubber connecting-sleeve on the small oil-feed pipe which projects from the base of the tank. If the gauze filter comes away with the rubber connecting-sleeve (1955-6) or feed pipe (1957-65), do not disturb it. If, however, the filter remains in the small pipe attached to the tank, grasp the ringed open end and pull the filter out of the pipe. Replace the filter in the reverse order of removal.

Note Concerning Oil Pipe Unions. The unions for the oil tank delivery and return pipes are very close to each other at the crankcase (*see* Fig. 21). When disconnecting an oil pipe be extremely careful not to allow the spanner to foul the union adjacent to the union from which the pipe is being disconnected. Carelessness in this matter can result in a *fractured crankcase*.

Removing Pump Plunger (1955-63 Models). Do not remove the oil-pump plunger unnecessarily. If you must remove it, first drain the oil tank as described on page 46. Also unscrew the union nut securing the bottom end of the oil-feed pipe from the pump housing to the rocker-box. Remove both end-caps from the pump housing by undoing the hexagon-headed securing bolts.

Just below the pump housing in front of the rear cap is the all-important guide screw and pin. Remove these together (*see* Fig. 20), and push out from the front the pump plunger and withdraw it from the rear end of the pump housing.

To Replace the Plunger. First make sure that the inside of the pump housing is clean, and check that the plunger itself is clean internally and externally. Oil the plunger and gently push it into position. Its smaller end must enter the rear of the pump housing, and the guide screw must next be fitted. Before replacing the guide screw, make certain that the steel pin inside the hollow screw is fitted as indicated in Fig. 20, or serious damage may be caused to the teeth of the pump plunger.

After replacing the guide screw, and while slowly tightening it, move the pump plunger backwards and forwards until the end of the guide-screw pin is felt to engage the profiled cam-groove at the rear end of the plunger.

When this happens, tighten the guide screw firmly, but on no account tighten before proper engagement is obtained, otherwise stripping of the teeth on the timing-side engine mainshaft and of the teeth on the plunger is liable to take place.

Fit the pump-housing front and rear end-caps and see that airtight joints are obtained. The two paper washers must be in perfect condition. Renew them if they are damaged in the slightest degree. Make certain when fitting the paper washer for the front end-cap that the small oil hole in the cap itself is not obstructed.

The Pump-housing End-caps. It is advisable to apply some liquid jointing compound to one side of each paper washer. This side must be fitted in contact with the end-cap. To ensure an airtight joint at each end-cap, it is essential to see that the securing bolts are tightened down evenly and firmly. Tightening should always be effected in a diagonal order. Also occasionally check the delivery and return-pipe union nuts for tightness.

The Gear-type Oil Pump (1964-5 Models). It should normally be quite unnecessary to disturb the gear-type oil pump as it is of very robust design. If you do dismantle the pump, when assembling it make sure that the end plates do not protrude over the pump body; they should be just below it. Note that the face of the oil pump body, where it joins the crankcase, must be absolutely flat and free from blemish and bruises. Otherwise the oil "pick up" from the pump will be reduced, as the pump will suck in air at this point. When fitting a gear-type oil pump apply a little Wellseal as jointing compound on the body of the pump.

Magneto Bearings (1955-7 Models). These are initially packed with grease by the makers during assembly and further greasing should not be necessary for 10,000-15,000 miles. When a general overhaul becomes necessary it is desirable to remove the magneto and return it to Joseph Lucas, Ltd. of Birmingham, 19, or to one of their service depots, for thorough servicing. No grease nipples are fitted, but the contact-breaker requires periodical oiling.

The Contact-breaker (1955-7 Magneto Models). On models fitted with a Lucas type SR-1 rotating-magnet magneto having automatic ignition-control mechanism on the driving side (behind a bulge on the magneto chain-case cover), about every 3,000 miles undo the three captive screws and remove the moulded end-cover. Then apply a spot of clean engine oil to the visible end of the contact-breaker pivot pin. About every 6,000 miles loosen the nut securing the contact-breaker spring and lift off the contact-breaker lever (*see* Fig. 29). The spring is slotted to facilitate

CORRECT LUBRICATION 49

removal. Then smear the pivot pin with a little Mobilgrease No. 2 or a similar grease.

Cam and Contact-breaker (1958–65 Models). On the 1958–65 coil-ignition models the Lucas CA1A type contact-breaker and the automatic ignition-advance mechanism are located inside the timing-case main cover. To obtain access to them, remove the two screws retaining the timing-case outer cover, and withdraw the latter (*see* Fig. 31).

About every 6,000 miles smear the surface of the cam very lightly with some Mobilgrease No. 2. If this is not available, use some clean *winter*-grade engine oil (*see* page 43). Also apply a spot of clean engine oil to the contact-breaker pivot. Squeeze a little grease into the felt wick.

Remove the central fixing bolt and inject a small quantity of clean engine oil into the exposed hole. After replacing the fixing bolt and running the engine for a few minutes, centrifugal force will force out the oil over the automatic ignition-advance mechanism.

The Magneto Chain (1955–7 Models). The magneto driving chain (enclosed in a chain case on the off-side of the engine) is not automatically lubricated like the dynamo chain. It is necessary to add some grease about every 2,000 miles. Suitable greases are Mobilgrease No. 2, Esso Fluid Grease, or Energrease A.O.

Remove the chain-case cover, and apply suitable grease generously to the chain. Also with a thin metal strip, work some of the grease well into the automatic ignition-control mechanism.

MOTOR-CYCLE LUBRICATION

The Dynamo Bearings (1955–7 Models). The armature bearings of the Lucas type E3LM dynamo, as on the magneto, are packed with grease by the makers on assembly and this should suffice for at least 10,000 miles running, or until it is necessary to make a general overhaul, when the dynamo should be removed and returned to Joseph Lucas, Ltd., or to a Lucas service depot for thorough cleaning, overhaul, and lubrication.

The Dynamo Driving Chain (1955–7). The Lucas dynamo is chain-driven from the engine shaft by a chain which is completely enclosed in the oil-bath chain case containing the primary chain. Therefore, provided the oil-bath chain case is kept properly replenished, no individual attention to the dynamo chain is necessary. The replenishment of the oil-bath is dealt with on page 51.

Gearbox Lubrication (1955–65). Matchless Motor Cycles, Ltd. advise the use of summer-grade engine oil (*see* page 43) for the four-speed heavyweight gearbox on the 1955–65 models.

Under normal conditions it is sufficient to check the oil level and if necessary top up the gearbox every 1,000 miles with summer-grade through the filler-cap orifice on the top edge of the kick-starter case cover. Excessive filling will result in leakage.

All 1955–6 Burman gearboxes and the 1957–65 A.M.C. gearboxes have an oil-level plug (3, Fig. 26) located close to the kick-starter spindle; to

FIG. 25. WHEN AND WHERE TO LUBRICATE (1955 ONWARDS)

The above lubrication chart (showing a 1957 Model 18S) applies to all 1955 and later O.H.V. singles, but note the following points: on 1955 models a different type oil tank (*see* Fig. 23) with fabric-type main filter is specified. On 1958–65 models with coil ignition no magneto is fitted, and on 1964–5 models "Roadholder" front forks are provided. (For key *see* opposite.)

top-up the gearbox to the maximum permissible level (content: 1 pt.), it is only necessary to pour in engine oil through the filler-cap orifice until it begins to trickle from the level-plug hole. On the 1955–6 Burman four-speed gearboxes the filler cap comprises a slotted and threaded circular-cap, but on the 1957–65 A.M.C. gearboxes the filler cap is replaced by a circular cover secured by two small screws. Removal of the circular cover, incidentally, gives access to the clutch thrust-mechanism.

Changing the Gearbox Oil. After the first 500 miles and thereafter about every 5,000 miles change the lubricant in the gearbox. The engine oil should be drained completely, the A.J.S. gearbox flushed out with a suitable flushing oil and afterwards replenished with 1 pint of summer-grade engine oil.

The screwed drain-plug is located low down at the rear of the gearbox shell. Before replenishing the gearbox make sure that the drain plug is replaced and firmly tightened.

CORRECT LUBRICATION

KEY TO FIG. 25

Item No.	Description of Item	Lubrication Required	Page Ref.
1	Oil tank	Before each run check oil circulation and level. Top-up as required. Every 5,000 miles change the oil and clean the filter(s). Also drain oil sump and clean sump filter.	44–7
2	Inlet-valve stem	If necessary, adjust the oil supply.	45
3	Contact-breaker (magneto and coil ignition)	Every 6,000 miles smear a little grease on the lever pivot-pin. On 1958–65 coil ignition models every 6,000 miles smear a little grease on the cam and apply a drop of engine oil to the contact-breaker pivot. Squeeze a little grease into the felt wick.	48–9
4	Magneto chain (1955–7)	Every 2,000 miles repack the chain with grease.	49
5	Gearbox	Every 1,000 miles top up with summer-grade engine oil to the correct level. Every 5,000 miles change the lubricant.	49–50
6	Primary chain	Every 500 miles check level in oil-bath and top up if necessary to inspection-cap orifice.	51
7	Secondary chain	Every 500 miles apply some grease or engine oil if dry. In wet weather, remove, clean, and grease every 2,000 miles.	52
8	Front and rear hubs	Every 1,000 miles apply the grease gun to the hub nipples where provided. Repack 1964–5 hub bearings every 10,000 miles.	53
9	The brakes	Every 1,000 miles apply the grease gun to the expander-bush nipples. Weekly oil the brake linkage.	54
10	Steering head	Every 1,000 miles grease both bearings with the grease gun.	54
11	Front-brake cable	Weekly oil the exposed end.	54
12	Rear-brake pedal	Every 3,000 miles apply the grease gun to the heel nipple.	54
13	Speedometer	Every 3,000 miles inject grease through the nipple on top of the speedometer gearbox.	54
14	Handlebar levers	Weekly apply a little oil to all moving parts. Inject some oil into the cables (where nipples are provided).	54
15	Stand	Occasionally oil fulcrum bolt.	55
16	Front forks	Every 5,000 miles (1955–63 models) check the hydraulic fluid content of both "Teledraulic legs," and top up if necessary. On 1964–5 models with "Roadholder" forks replenish at 10,000-mile intervals each fork leg with 5 fluid ounces of damping oil.	55–7
17	Spring frame	Occasionally grease 1957–65 Girling cam-ring adjusters.	57

Primary Chain Lubrication. Remove the inspection cap from the oil-bath chain case about every 500 miles and observe the level of oil. On no account must the oil level be permitted to fall below $\frac{3}{16}$ in. from the bottom edge of the inspection-cap orifice, with the machine standing vertically on level ground. The correct amount of oil is present when its surface is just below the bottom edge of the inspection orifice.*

* The bottom chain run should be just in contact with the oil.

If the oil level is too low, some harshness in the primary transmission generally develops, except on 1957–65 models where a sliding oil seal in the form of two steel discs surrounds the gearbox mainshaft. Top up the oil-bath chain case as required and when necessary, using one of the brands of the summer-grade oils mentioned on page 43. Lubrication must not be neglected, for the oil-bath is responsible for lubricating: (*a*) the primary

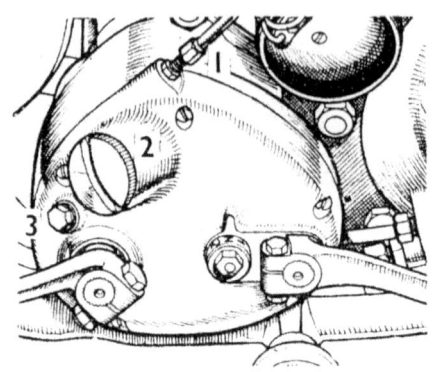

FIG. 26. THE 1955–6 BURMAN GEARBOX
(*By courtesy of "Motor Cycle"—London*)

KEY TO FIG. 26

1. Clutch-cable adjuster. 2. Filler cap. 3. Oil-level plug.

chain, (*b*) the dynamo chain, and (*c*) the engine shaft shock-absorber. (*b*) and (*c*) are omitted on 1958–65 models.

Oil-bath Inspection Cap Removal (1955–7). To remove the cap, unscrew the knurled screw approximately *four turns*. Then slide the cap sideways until it is possible to slip the back plate through the orifice and remove the complete cap assembly.

To prevent the risk of the filler cap, or inspection cap, being lost while riding, it is important to centralize the cork washer before firmly tightening the knurled retaining screw. Do not forget this when replacing the inspection cap.

Oil-bath Inspection Cap Removal (1958–65). On 1958–65 models with an aluminium oil-bath chain case, to remove the inspection cap apply the appropriate spanner (Part No. 018178) to the slot machined in the screwed cap.

Secondary Chain Lubrication. About every 500 miles examine the condition of the secondary chain. If the chain is in a dry state, turn the

CORRECT LUBRICATION

rear wheel by hand and apply some grease or engine oil with a brush or oil-can. About every 2,000 miles (except where the chain is fully enclosed) it is advisable to remove the chain from the sprockets and clean and lubricate it in the following manner—
(1) Clean the chain thoroughly with paraffin.
(2) Hang up the chain and allow to dry.
(3) Immerse the chain for at least *ten minutes* in a suitable receptacle containing Mobilgrease No. 2, B.P. Energrease A.O., Esso Fluid Grease, or Castrolease Grease Graphited. The grease should be heated until just fluid and maintained in this state during the period of chain immersion.
(4) Hang up the chain to drain off surplus grease.

Having lubricated the chain, fit it to the gearbox and rear-wheel sprockets. It is permissible to lubricate the chain, using engine oil instead of one of the greases mentioned, but this substitute is not so good. Allow the chain to soak for several hours where engine oil is used.

Recommended Greases to Use. For hub lubrication and the lubrication of all frame parts having grease nipples the following greases are recommended by the makers of A.J.S. motor-cycles: Castrolease Heavy, MP Mobilgrease, Shell Retinax A or C.D., Energrease C3, or Regent Marfax. The grease must, of course, be applied with a grease gun to the nipples provided on the machine.

Filling Grease Gun. The grease gun (Part No. 017246) provided with the tool kit must be applied periodically to all grease nipples provided on the machine.

Suitable greases to use for various motor-cycle parts are those recommended above. The grease gun must be charged so that the grease is on the *top* side of the piston. Special grease canisters are available with loose collars provided with holes. To charge the grease gun from one of these canisters, place the barrel of the gun over the hole in the central floating plate and press downwards firmly. Turn the grease gun and at the same time remove it from the floating plate. This should charge the grease gun so that the grease is flush with the top of the barrel. Having charged the grease gun, replace its screwed-top cap. If no grease canister of the type referred to is available, charge the grease gun by hand, using a suitable lath or similar implement.

The Wheel Hubs (1955–62 Models). On new machines the hubs of both wheels are packed with grease. To prevent mud and water entering the hubs, and to ensure correct lubrication, inject some grease through the nipple through the hole in the hub disc of each hub about every 1,000 miles. Avoid excessive lubrication, or some of the grease may get on to the brake linings and impair the efficiency of the brakes. 1964–5 hub bearings are packed with grease (*see* page 54).

The Wheel Hubs (1963–5 Models). The hubs have no grease nipples provided. The hub bearings on new machines are packed with sufficient grease for about 10,000 miles. Subsequently about every 10,000 miles remove both wheels (*see* pages 119–21), dismantle the hubs, and clean and repack their bearings with fresh grease (*see* pages 123 onwards).

Steering-head Lubrication. Apply the grease gun sparingly to the grease nipple in the head lug of the frame about every 1,000 miles. Also grease the nipple (where fitted) on the right-hand side of the handlebar lug.

The Front and Rear Brakes. Inject a little grease about every 1,000 miles through a grease nipple provided on each brake cover-plate for the expander bush. About every 3,000 miles apply the grease gun to the nipple in the heel of the rear-brake pedal.

Smear a few drops of engine oil *weekly* on the yoke-end pins at the front and rear ends of the rear-brake rod. Do not forget the threaded portion of the rod to which the hand adjuster is fitted. Also remember the exposed end of the front-brake cable.

Speedometer-Gearbox Lubrication. To ensure smooth and efficient running, grease the speedometer gearbox every 3,000 miles. The gearbox is attached to the rear-wheel spindle and the grease nipple is located on top of the speedometer gearbox. No further lubrication is required beyond the above-mentioned attention.

The Throttle Twist-grip. Stiffness sometimes develops and this spoils sensitive control of the throttle. To rectify stiffness is quite simple, and the following procedure should be adopted—

(1) Remove both the screws which retain the halves of the twist-grip clip.
(2) Withdraw the twist-grip from the end of the handlebars.
(3) Smear some grease on the off-side part of the handlebars over which the twist-grip fits.
(4) Smear some grease on the friction spring, and also on the drum on which the internal wire is wound.
(5) Replace the twist-grip on the end of the handlebars.
(6) Fit the two screws retaining the halves of the twist-grip clip and firmly tighten the screws.

The Handlebar Levers. It is advisable to apply a little engine oil *weekly* to all the moving parts of the handlebar levers. This will reduce friction and keep the controls responsive and easy to operate.

On most 1955–7 models the control cables for the throttle slide and clutch lever have a conveniently situated nipple for the injection of engine oil by means of a grease gun. Some engine oil should be injected at the

CORRECT LUBRICATION 55

first indication of jerky or stiff action. When using the gun, hold it as nearly vertical as possible, with the nozzle facing *downward*.

The Stand. Occasionally lubricate the stand hinge bolt; apply some engine oil with an oil-can. There are several small parts on the machine where only a little movement occurs. All such parts should be similarly lubricated. This will facilitate free movement and prevent rusting. The main parts of the A.J.S. requiring attention are indicated in the lubrication chart on page 50.

Sidecar Chassis. Do not forget to lubricate a sidecar chassis. Several grease nipples are provided for the purpose.

Hydraulic Fluids for "Teledraulic" Front Forks (1955–63). The "Teledraulic" front forks require no actual lubrication. It is necessary, however, occasionally to check the hydraulic fluid content of each fork leg ($6\frac{1}{2}$ fluid ounces); top-up if necessary, as described in later paragraphs of this chapter. Below are specified suitable types of fluid for the A.J.S. hydraulic dampers—
(1) Wakefield's "Castrolite" (SAE-20).
(2) Mobiloil "Arctic" (SAE-20).
(3) Shell X-100 Motor Oil 20/20W (SAE-20).
(4) B.P. Energol SAE-20.
(5) Essolube "20" (SAE-20).

Hydraulic Fluid Content (1955–63 "Teledraulic" Front Forks). It is wise every 5,000 miles to check the hydraulic-fluid content of each front-fork leg. Before beginning this check, it is necessary to see that your A.J.S. is quite vertical, with the weight on both wheels. Place a suitable box beneath each footrest. Remove the two hexagon-headed plugs from the tops of the fork-leg inner tubes, after levering off (1955) the snap-on dome caps, or removing the rubber grommets (1956–63).

To determine the fluid content of each fork leg, remove the drain plug from the base of the fork-leg slider and permit the hydraulic fluid to drain off into a graduated measuring jug or other vessel having a capacity of at least 10 fluid ounces. Most of the fluid will drain off, but not all of it will do so.

Replace the drain plug in the base of the fork-leg slider on 1955–7 models. On these models the damper rod is attached to the hexagon-headed plug at the top of each fork leg and it is necessary to work each damper rod up and down, employing a pumping action. Hold the top plug with the fingers only, and make very sharp *upward* strokes. Wait two minutes and then remove the drain plug a second time and catch any further hydraulic fluid which may drain off into the graduated vessel already containing most of the fluid.

It may be necessary to repeat the 1955–7 draining procedure (including working the top plugs up and down) several times to ensure that the maximum quantity of hydraulic fluid is drained off into the graduated vessel. Note the total amount of fluid extracted. It is not possible to extract in this manner the whole content of each leg (6½ fluid ounces), but the amount drained off and measured should total 6 fluid ounces.

Topping-up (1955–63 "Teledraulic" Front Forks). The checking of the hydraulic-fluid content and the topping-up of each fork leg should be effected in one continuous operation. Deal with each fork leg individually. It is assumed that the fluid content of the leg has already been determined. Then top-up as follows—
(1) If the total amount of hydraulic fluid extracted from the fork leg measured exactly 6 fluid ounces, no topping-up is necessary. If the amount is less than the appropriate quantity just stated, add hydraulic fluid (of the type already in use) to the graduated vessel until the total amount of fluid measures exactly 6 fluid ounces.
(2) Replace the drain plug in the base of the fork slider.
(3) Pour the 6 fluid ounces contained in the graduated vessel into the top of the fork inner-tube.
(4) Replace the hexagon-headed top plug (and rubber washer), and firmly tighten the plug. Also replace the snap-on dome cap (1955) or rubber grommet (1956–63).
It is important to note that where 1955–63 "Teledraulic" front forks have been completely stripped down (necessarily incurring the removal of *all* hydraulic fluid), it is essential after assembly to top-up each fork leg with 6½ fluid ounces, not the quantity (½ fluid ounce less) just quoted for topping-up.

Replenishing 1964–5 "Roadholder" Front Forks. These telescopic front forks are of entirely different design to the 1955–63 "Teledraulic" forks, but the same type of damping oils referred to on page 53 are suitable. The normal oil content is 5 fluid ounces (142 c.c.). The damping oil should be drained and replenished after the first 1,000 miles and subsequently at 10,000-mile intervals or whenever the normal characteristics of the forks appear to have deteriorated.
The fork springs abut against the filler plugs and therefore before removing these plugs it is essential to take the weight off the front wheel by placing the machine on its central stand. Otherwise the forks are likely to collapse. With the machine on its central stand unscrew the two top hexagon-headed filler plugs. Now place a suitable receptacle to catch oil draining off from the fork leg first to be dealt with. Remove the drain plug screw. This is the small screw on the rear side at the bottom of the fork leg. Be careful not to lose the small washer for the drain plug. Allow all oil to drain off. Draining is assisted by tilting the wheel to one side.

Drain the other fork leg in a similar manner. Finally replenish both fork legs after replacing both drain plugs and their washers. See that the drain plugs are firmly tightened. Use a measured container to pour in 5 fluid ounces of damping oil into the top of each fork leg. Afterwards replace the two filler plugs and their washers. Note that the air-space between the fork springs and the insides of the tubes is very small and replenishment must be done with extreme care to avoid loss of oil by spilling.

The "Swinging Arm." The "swinging arm" assembly in whose rear end the rear wheel is mounted is hinged just behind the gearbox, and the "swinging arm" fork-hinge plain bearings (*see* Fig. 3) are automatically lubricated from a reservoir containing $1\frac{1}{2}$ fluid ounces (42·6 c.c.) of heavy gear oil. This should suffice to lubricate the bearings for an almost indefinite period. Slight oil leakage may occur on a new machine (or where the reservoir has been replenished), but this is of no significance and stops after a few hundred miles have been covered. If replenishment should ever become necessary, remove the small screw from the off-side hinge bearing-cap and top-up the oil reservoir with heavy gear oil (S.A.E. 140) to the level of the screw orifice.

"Teledraulic" Rear-Suspension Units (1955–6). The rear-suspension units have hydraulic damping springs of almost identical design to that used for the "Teledraulic" front forks. But only if leakage of hydraulic fluid occurs (most unlikely) is it necessary to replenish the fork legs with the correct amount of fluid. Should the leg action become excessively lively, it is possible that some loss of damping fluid is responsible, but unless you are in serious doubt as to the correct functioning of the rear-suspension units, you are advised to leave well alone.

The correct fluids to use are those specified on page 55. Each fork leg should contain exactly 85 c.c. or a little below 3 fluid ounces. On no account must the oil content exceed 90 c.c.

Girling Rear-Suspension Units (1957–65). These proprietary units are sealed by the makers and do not require to be topped-up. During initial assembly their springs are lubricated and sufficient hydraulic fluid inserted in the damper units to last until the Girling units require to be renewed.

Occasionally clean and grease the cam-ring adjusters provided to give three different spring tensions. If the movement of the telescopic legs is accompanied by a rubbing noise or squeaking, remove the two half circlips securing each top cover-tube, remove the unit top fixing bolt, remove the tube, and apply some grease to the outside diameter of the spring.

CHAPTER V

GENERAL MAINTENANCE

THIS chapter contains full maintenance instructions for all 1955–65 touring singles. Some instructions, however, have already been included in Chapters II–IV. Appropriate cross-references to these earlier chapters are therefore also included.

A.J.S. Repairs and Spares. When you have occasion to forward or deliver parts to the manufacturers* (either for repair or as patterns) always attach to *each* part a label on which is written clearly your full name and address. To ensure quick attention, all correspondence concerning spares and technical advice should be written on separate sheets, each bearing your name and address.

Always quote the *complete* engine number which will be found on the near-side of the crankcase. Also state the model concerned.

There are numerous firms in the United Kingdom who can supply A.J.S. spares over the counter, and many who specialize in the repair of engines and machines. Useful addresses may be found in the advertisement pages of *Motor Cycle* and *Motor Cycling*. If taking a machine to Plumstead, first make an appointment (Woolwich 1223).

Some London Accessory Firms. Among reputable London firms (some of which have provincial branches) handling motor-cycle accessories, equipment spares, tools, clothing, etc. may be mentioned: Whitbys of Acton, Ltd.; Claude Rye, Ltd.; E. S. Motors; The Halford Cycle Co., Ltd.; Turner's Stores; James Grose, Ltd.; Marble Arch Motor Supplies, Ltd.; Pride & Clarke, Ltd.; and George Grose, Ltd.

ENGINE MAINTENANCE

Items for Maintenance. For engine maintenance there are certain items which you *must* have handy in the lock-up or garage. These include: a can of paraffin for cleaning purposes; a stiff brush for scouring dirt off the crankcase; a tin of suitable engine oil (*see* page 43); a canister of grease; a small oil-can containing some engine oil; a receptacle for oil when draining the oil tank and oil sump; a pail or some jars for washing engine parts in; some non-fluffy rags; valve-grinding paste such as Richford's (coarse

---

* The A.J.S. Service and Repair Dept. is in Burrage Grove, Plumstead, London, S.E. 18.

and fine); some fine emery cloth; a set of paper washers and gaskets (*see* illustrated Spares List); some jointing compound; a pair of new gudgeon-pin circlips; and some good hand cleanser, such as "Gre-solvent."

Tools Required. The A.J.S. tool kit is adequate for any normal stripping down and assembly job and should prove sufficient for routine maintenance and overhaul. It is also necessary for maintenance to obtain a suitable feeler gauge for checking the sparking plug gap (*see* page 61), an A.J.S. valve-spring compressor (for 1955 and subsequent engines with hairpin valve springs), and a valve holder for grinding-in the valves. The Part Nos. are 018276 and 017482 respectively. It is also desirable to obtain a wire brush for cleaning sparking plugs.

Should you decide to undertake as much repair work as possible in addition to routine maintenance, stripping-down, and assembly, it is desirable to rig up a suitable bench, complete with vice, and to purchase some extra tools (various A.J.S. service tools are available).

To begin, it is a good plan to buy a medium-weight hammer, a hand-drill and an assortment of twist-drills, a hacksaw, some large and small (smooth and rough) files, and a good soldering outfit for the repair of control cables. Repair work is beyond the scope of this handbook, and you are not advised to tackle such work unless you have fair technical knowledge, skill in handling tools, and good facilities.

Engine Lubrication. Detailed instructions on lubricating the A.J.S. engine are given in Chapter IV. Attend to lubrication points 1 to 4 indicated in the Lubrication Chart on page 50.

The Amal Carburettor. For comprehensive advice on how to maintain correct carburation, refer to the instructions given in Chapter II.

Keep your Engine Clean. Keep your engine clean externally as well as internally. By so doing you enhance pride of ownership and obtain other advantages. Dirt is apt to mask defects and can accidentally enter the engine when it is being stripped down. It will also make rusting more likely. Rusted cylinder fins, besides being an eyesore, are detrimental to efficient dispersion of heat by radiation. They should be clean and black. On the A.J.S. they are stove enamelled black (1955 and later models have light-alloy cylinder heads).

To clean the cylinder and cylinder-head fins, use a stiff brush dipped in paraffin. If the stove-enamelling has worn away, paint the fins with a good proprietary cylinder black. Clean the aluminium alloy and bright surfaces with rags and paraffin, assisted by brushes where necessary, and scour off the filth from the lower part of the crankcase by means of stiff brushes and paraffin. Thorough cleaning may take some time, but it is well worth while.

Check Nuts for Tightness Occasionally. On a new A.J.S. where some initial bedding-down occurs, it is advisable to check all external nuts and bolts for tightness fairly frequently. After the running-in period is completed it is a good habit to check the external nuts regularly every 3,000 miles. Pay special attention to the cylinder nuts, the nuts on the engine plates, and the union nuts for the pipe connexions. Do not over-tighten.

SPARKING PLUGS, CONTACT-BREAKER, ETC.

The ignition system comprises: a 14 mm sparking plug; a Lucas rotating-magnet type magneto (1955–7 models), with automatic ignition-control mechanism on the driving side; or a Lucas type CA1A contact-breaker unit with automatic timing control (1958 onwards). The contact-breaker unit and timing control are both housed in the timing case of the 1958 and later coil-ignition models. They are operated from the inlet camshaft, and a coil is clipped to the frame top tube underneath the petrol tank. Current is taken from the battery through the contact-breaker unit to the ignition coil (unless the ignition key is in the "EMG" position).

Suitable Sparking Plugs. To obtain maximum engine performance throughout the throttle range, plus easy starting, it is essential always to run on a suitable type of sparking plug. Three reliable makes of sparking plugs are the K.L.G., the Lodge, and the Champion. Suitable (14 mm thread and ¾ in. reach) types are—

K.L.G.—Fit a three-point, detachable type FE80, or else the appropriate watertight version.

LODGE—Fit a three-point, detachable type HLN or a type HLNP on all 1955 and later models.

CHAMPION—Fit a non-detachable type N-5 (all 1955 and later models).

For regular bad-weather riding it is advisable to fit a weather-proof terminal cover to the plug, or else to use a watertight plug corresponding to the appropriate non-watertight plugs recommended above. It is necessary according to law to fit an ignition-suppression type plug, or a terminal cover with built-in suppressor, so as not to annoy users of wireless and television sets. Note that ignition-suppression type plugs have longer-wearing electrodes.

Be Careful When Removing a Plug. If considerable resistance is felt when removing a sparking plug with the A.J.S. box spanner and tommy bar, apply some penetrating oil to the plug threads. Do not forget that on 1955 and later models the cylinder head is made of a light alloy and the plug threads can be damaged if excessive force is used to remove the sparking plug. A cylinder head costs considerably more than a sparking plug!

GENERAL MAINTENANCE

The Sparking Plug Gap. It is advisable to check the gap between the electrodes of the sparking plug about every 3,000 miles. The correct gap is 0·020–0·022 in., and it is advisable to re-gap the plug if burning of the points has increased the gap to over 0·22 in. When re-gapping a plug it is desirable for obvious reasons to set its gap at or near the *bottom* limit.

Check the gap with a suitable feeler gauge (a wire gauge if the points are not very accessible). The gauge should be a nice sliding fit. When adjusting the gap, never attempt to bend or tap the centre electrode. Use a plug re-gapping tool (*see* Fig. 27) or a small pair of snipe-nose pliers,

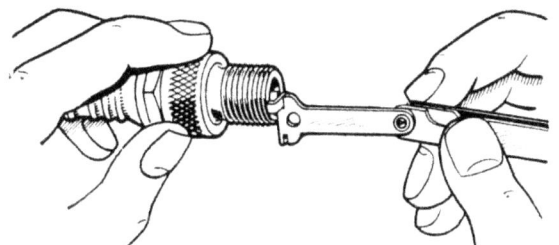

FIG. 27. THE BEST WAY TO RE-GAP A PLUG

to bend the outside (earth) electrode(s). Tapping the outer electrode(s) inwards to reduce the gap is permissible, if the plug is held in a vice and a light hammer and copper drift are used. When the plug has to be thoroughly cleaned, this should be done as described below, and the plug re-gapped *afterwards*.

Cleaning the Sparking Plug. If carburation is quite satisfactory and excessive oil is not entering the combustion chamber, it should not be necessary to dismantle and clean the sparking plug thoroughly more often than once about every 3,000 miles. When running-in a new or rebored engine, however, it is advisable to remove and check the plug for cleanliness at intervals of about 500 miles.

Quick cleaning of a plug can be done by brushing the points and lightly rubbing their firing sides with some smooth emery-cloth. Thorough cleaning (internal and external), however, is not possible without dismantling the plug (*see* below).

To Clean K.L.G. and Lodge Plugs. Fig. 28 shows a typical detachable type (K.L.G.) sparking plug dismantled for thorough cleaning. To dismantle a detachable-type plug, grip the smaller hexagon on the gland nut (*B*) in a vice, with the plug upside down. Be most careful not to exert any pressure on the hexagon faces. Then with the plug box-spanner, or a suitable ring spanner, unscrew the large hexagon (*E*) on the plug body. Alternatively use two spanners to unscrew the gland nut from the plug body. The centre electrode (*F*) with its insulation, comprising the insulated electrode assembly (*A*), can now be detached from the gland nut. Take care not to lose the internal sealing washer (*H*).

To clean the insulation, wipe it clean with a cloth soaked in petrol or paraffin. If the insulation is coated with hard carbon deposit, remove these with some fairly coarse glass-paper and wash again, but make no attempt to scrape off the deposits. The internal sealing washer (*H*) and the surfaces on the insulator, and in the metal body on which this washer rests, are very important as they prevent gas-leakage through the plug. Therefore wipe them only with a rag soaked in petrol or paraffin. Any damage caused while dismantling will render the plug unserviceable.

To clean the metal parts (plug body and gland nut), wipe them clean with petrol, and, if necessary, scrape off the deposits with a small knife, or use a wire brush. Afterwards rinse the parts in petrol. The gland nut seldom gets very fouled, but the inside of the plug body may be very dirty, and the same may apply to the external threads of the plug. Clean and polish the points (see Fig. 28) of the centre and outside (earth) electrodes (*F*) and (*G*) with some fine emery cloth.

See that there is no dirt or grit lodged between the body of the plug and the insulation, and particularly on the internal sealing-washer and all contacting faces. Smear a little thin oil on the internal washer and make sure that it seats properly. When assembling the sparking plug, see that the centre electrode and insulation are positioned centrally in the body bore. If not, remove, re-position by rotating the centre a quarter of a turn, and re-assemble. Do not attempt to force into position or bend.

Tighten the gland nut into the plug body just sufficiently to give a gas-tight joint. Do not use an open-ended spanner. Finally verify that the plug gap is correct.

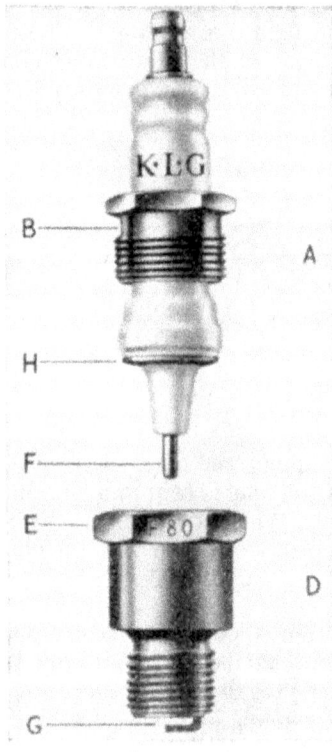

FIG. 28. DETACHABLE TYPE SPARKING PLUG (K.L.G.) DISMANTLED FOR THOROUGH CLEANING

The gland nut *B* and the internal washer *H* are shown still in position on the insulation.

GENERAL MAINTENANCE

To Clean Champion Plugs. A Champion non-detachable plug such as the N-5 cannot be dismantled and cleaned like the detachable-type Lodge and K.L.G. plugs. Quick cleaning is of course done in the same manner (see page 61). The best method of cleaning a Champion plug thoroughly is to take it to a nearby garage having an "air-blast" unit. In a matter of a few minutes the plug can be thoroughly cleaned of all deposits, washed, and tested for sparking at a pressure exceeding 100 lb. per sq. in.

To assist cleaning, use a small wire brush. Wipe the tip and outside of the insulation thoroughly clean. After removing all carbon, polish the electrodes with some fine emery cloth. Finally, check the plug gap (0·020 in.–0·022 in.).

Fitting a Plug. Before replacing the plug, renew the copper washer if it is worn or flattened, and clean the plug threads. It is a good plan to coat the threads with some graphite paste or "Oil Dag" before replacing the plug. Screw the plug home by hand as far as possible, and always use the plug spanner in the tool kit for final tightening. The use of excessive force is undesirable and can cause distortion and possibly damage the cylinder-head threads.

To Check Contact-breaker Gap (1955–7 Models). On all 1955–7 models it is advisable after the first 500 miles to remove the moulded cover from the Lucas type S.R.-1 rotating-magnet magneto and check the gap between the contacts of the contact-breaker. It is subsequently sufficient to check the gap at intervals of about 3,000 miles. Actual adjustment is seldom needed. The correct contact-breaker gap is 0·010 in.–0·012 in.

The correct procedure for checking the contact-breaker gap is as follows—

(1) Remove the contact-breaker cover and rotate the engine slowly forwards until the contacts of the contact-breaker are wide open.

(2) Insert the blade of the feeler gauge (attached to the magneto spanner) between the contacts.

(3) If the feeler gauge *just* slides in without friction, the gap is correct and no adjustment is needed. If the gauge is a slack fit or the contacts have to be sprung to enable it to enter, adjust the gap as below.

Should an adjustment of the contact-breaker gap be necessary, slacken the two securing screws (see Fig. 29) holding the fixed contact plate and move the plate as required until the gap is correct. Having made the required adjustment, firmly tighten the two securing-screws, again check the gap, and finally replace the moulded cover. Tighten its three fixing-screws firmly.

To Check Contact-breaker Gap (1958 Onwards). On the 1958 and later models check the contact-breaker gap after covering 500 miles on a new machine, and thereafter regularly about every 3,000 miles.

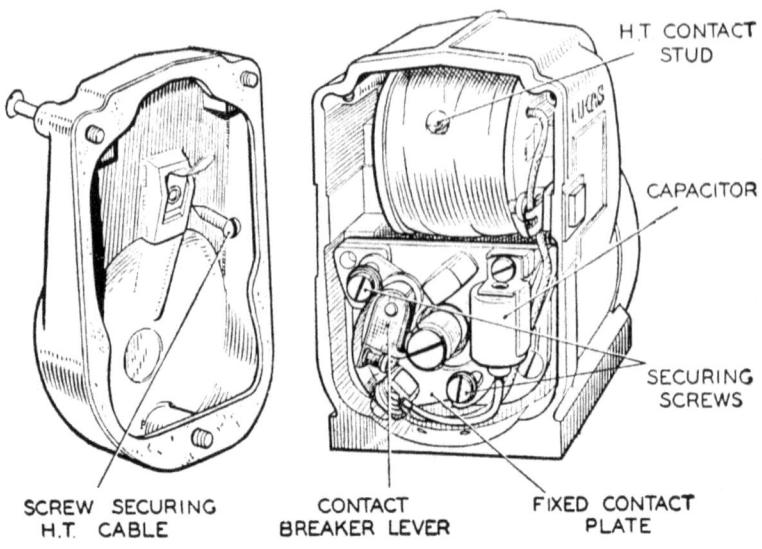

FIG. 29. CONTACT-BREAKER END OF LUCAS ROTATING-MAGNET MAGNETO (1955–7)

This magneto has automatic ignition-control mechanism on its driving side.

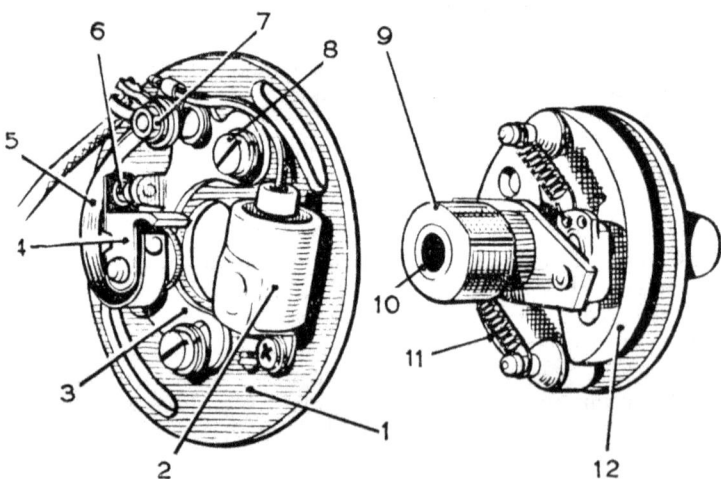

FIG. 30. THE CONTACT-BREAKER (LEFT) AND AUTOMATIC IGNITION-TIMING CONTROL (RIGHT) UNITS REMOVED FROM THE TIMING-CASE COVER AND INLET CAMSHAFT OF A COIL-IGNITION MODEL (1958–65)

1. Contact-breaker plate (fixed).
2. Capacitor.
3. Contact plate (adjustable).
4. Contact-breaker lever.
5. Spring for 4.
6. Contacts.
7. Terminal nut.
8. Securing screw (one of two) for 1.
9. Cam operating contact-breaker.
10. Hole for bolt securing timing-control unit.
11. Spring (one of two) controlling bob weight.
12. Bob weight (one of two).

GENERAL MAINTENANCE 65

To check the contact-breaker gap, first remove the two screws securing the outer cover to the timing case, and remove the cover. Next turn the engine over slowly until the contacts are fully open. Then insert a suitable feeler gauge between the contacts and check the gap which should be 0·14 in.–0·16 in. If the correct size feeler gauge just slides in without friction, the gap is correct and no adjustment is needed. If an adjustment is required, make it as described below.

With the engine still in the position where the maximum contact gap is obtained, loosen the two screws which secure the fixed contact plate (see Fig. 30). Then adjust the position of the plate as required until the gap between the contacts is correct. Afterwards fully tighten the two plate-securing screws.

Cleaning the Contact-breaker. The contact-breaker, especially the contacts themselves, must *never* be permitted to get dirty or oily; otherwise ignition trouble will inevitably ensue, and the contacts will become burned and pitted. When checking the gap of the contact-breaker, *always* inspect the contacts closely and, if they need cleaning, do this *before* finally adjusting the gap. Normally clean every 6,000 miles.

If the contacts have a *grey, frosted* appearance, it can be reasonably assumed that they are fairly healthy. Should they be only slightly discoloured, clean both contacts with a cloth moistened with petrol. Where the contacts are pitted or blackened, they must be thoroughly cleaned with a fine carborundum stone or, if one is not available, *very fine* emery cloth. Afterwards all metallic dust and dirt must be completely removed with a petrol-moistened cloth. Cleaning is simplified by removing the lever carrying the moving contact (see below).

When cleaning and dressing the contacts, it is essential to remove the minimum amount of contact metal necessary to ensure: (*a*) brightness of the contacts, (*b*) parallelism of the contacts, (*c*) perfect smoothness and truth of contact faces. To ensure this it is advisable to withdraw the moving contact.

To Withdraw Moving Contact (1955–7). On 1955–7 models with a rotating-magnet type magneto, to remove the contact-breaker lever (see Fig. 29) carrying the moving contact, remove the nut securing the end of the contact-breaker spring. The spring is slotted to permit of easy withdrawal of the lever.

To Withdraw Moving Contact (1958–65). To withdraw the moving contact on 1958 and later models having coil ignition, unscrew the nut which secures the end of the spring (*see* Fig. 30) and remove the nut, spring washer, and bush. Then lift the contact-breaker lever carrying the moving contact off its pivot.

To Renew h.t. Cable (1955–7 Models). Where a Lucas rotating-magnet type SR-1 magneto is fitted, 7 mm. rubber-covered ignition cable is also required for renewal purposes. To connect to the magneto, first remove the moulded cover from the contact-breaker side, and unscrew the pointed screw (*see* Fig. 29) from the back of the cover. Pull out the old ignition cable and push the new cable right home. Then secure the cable by tightening the pointed screw. Its point will penetrate the insulation and ensure good electrical contact with the core of the cable.

Testing the h.t. Cable. If the engine is running well, obviously the cable is sound but, if the engine refuses to start, it is desirable to ascertain whether the h.t. current is reaching the plug end of the cable. Place the steel blade of a *wooden-handled* screwdriver in contact with the plug terminal and almost in contact with one of the cylinder fins. Kick the engine over smartly and note whether a "fat" spark occurs. If it does, the cable is sound, but if it does not the cable or magneto is at fault.

To Re-tension Magneto Chain (1955–7 Models). About every 3,000 miles remove the cover from the magneto chain-case and inspect the chain for tension. Some stretching occurs, especially on a new chain, and where this is excessive it may spoil the exact ignition-timing and accelerate wear of the chain and sprockets. Press the magneto chain-run up and down (in its *tautest* position) midway between the magneto and camshaft sprockets. If the tension is correct, the *total* deflection should not exceed approximately $\frac{1}{4}$ in. If it is appreciably more or less, re-tension the chain as described below. Over-tensioning may damage the magneto.

(1) Loosen the nut on the rear of two bolts which support and secure the adjustable magneto-platform.

(2) Insert the blade of a screwdriver beneath the rear end of the magneto platform and prise it upwards until the correct chain tension is obtained.

(3) Tighten firmly the single nut on the magneto-platform rear securing bolt.

(4) Again check the tension of the driving chain.

(5) Grease the chain if necessary (*see* page 49) and fit the cover to the chain-case. Do not use jointing compound. Tighten the various cover securing-screws evenly.

Automatic Ignition-control Mechanism (1955–7). The control mechanism on the driving side of the Lucas type SR-1 rotating magnet magneto requires no adjustment, but the mechanism should be greased (*see* page 49) when greasing the magneto chain.

Automatic Ignition-control Unit Removal (1958–65). Normally the unit requires no attention other than occasional lubrication (*see* page 49). Removal is therefore unlikely to be necessary unless the renewal of some part is required after an extremely big mileage. Removal is necessary, however, as a preliminary to retiming the ignition on coil-ignition models. The following is the correct procedure.

First remove the outer cover from the timing case after removing the two securing nuts. Next remove the two securing screws which pass through slotted holes in the fixed contact-breaker plate (*see* Fig. 30) and remove the plate. Then remove the central bolt which secures the timing-control unit to a taper on the inlet camshaft. Fit a withdrawal bolt (Part No. 024328) in place of the bolt removed, and tighten slightly. Now direct a sharp tap on the end of the withdrawal bolt. This will free the ignition-control unit from the inlet camshaft extension and enable it to be withdrawn.

Do not interfere with the detachable contact-breaker cam which is rotated by two pegs engaged in the plates for the control springs. Should for some reason the cam be removed, note its position prior to removal.

TIMING THE MAGNETO (1955–7 MODELS)

The Correct Magneto-timing. Incorrect magneto-timing can have a most detrimental effect on the engine, besides reducing its performance. A late timing will result in a "woolly" engine and a hot and noisy exhaust, with considerable overheating and inability to develop full power. An early timing, on the other hand, may result in the engine being powerful on the larger throttle openings, but it will have a nasty tendency to kick-back when being started and it will "knock" readily under slight provocation. Worst of all, the engine will be subjected to some fuel detonation and stresses for which it is *not* designed.

Never attempt to improve on the maker's timing, which is such that *the contact-breaker contacts begin to open with the piston $\frac{1}{2}$ in. before T.D.C. on the compression stroke.* Sometimes it is necessary for some reason to remove the magneto or its driving chain. Where this is done, the magneto must be re-timed. For this purpose it is desirable to have available the following two items—

(*a*) A stout screwdriver, or an old-type tyre lever with the end turned up.

(*b*) A small rod or stout wheel spoke about $5\frac{1}{2}$ in. long.

1. Timing the Magneto—Preliminaries. Remove the covers from (*a*) the contact-breaker, (*b*) the off-side of the rocker-box, and (*c*) the magneto chain-case. Also remove the plug. Check first that the gap at the contact-breaker is correct (0·010 in.–0·012 in.) as described on page 63. It is also advisable to check that the magneto chain is correctly tensioned. The contact-breaker gap *must* be correct, as this affects the timing appreciably.

Loosen by several turns the nut which secures the magneto-driving sprocket to the camshaft, but do not take the nut right off. Then, with the stout screwdriver or the tyre lever referred to above, placed behind the sprocket, lever the latter off the taper on the camshaft. Rotate the engine forwards slowly until the piston is at true T.D.C. with *both valves closed*, as described below.

2. Finding the Exact Piston Position. Slip the $5\frac{1}{2}$ in. length of rod through the hole for the sparking plug. Rotate the engine *forwards* slowly until it is felt that the piston is exactly at the top of its stroke. In this position no movement is imparted to the rod. Without moving the piston, mark the rod flush with the top face of the sparking-plug hole. Remove the rod and scratch another mark $\frac{1}{2}$ in. above the first. Again insert the rod through the sparking-plug hole and slowly turn the engine *backwards* by means of the rear wheel (with top gear engaged) until the upper of the two marks on the rod is flush with the top of the sparking-plug hole; $\frac{1}{2}$ in. equals 39 deg. before T.D.C.

3. Timing the Contact "Break." Turn (with the finger and thumb) *to the maximum extent possible* the front plate of the automatic ignition-control mechanism. This is its fully advanced position. Lock the control in this position by inserting a small wooden wedge. Without moving the piston, rotate the sprocket secured to the magneto armature-shaft (and the driving chain) *anti-clockwise*, viewed from the driving side, until the contacts of the contact-breaker are just beginning to open.

To determine the exact moment of the "break," insert a thin cellophane slip between the contacts and exert a gentle pull on the paper when the magneto sprocket is being slowly turned.

When the exact position of the "break" has been found, secure the sprocket to the camshaft, being most careful not to permit the camshaft and/or armature to move while tightening the camshaft nut.

Finally check over the magneto timing again, verify the chain tension, grease the chain (*see* page 49) if necessary, and replace the covers for the contact-breaker, rocker-box, and magneto chain-case. Before replacing the magneto chain-case cover do not forget to remove the wooden wedge previously used to lock the automatic ignition-control mechanism in the fully advanced position. Fit the sparking plug and you should be "all set."

TIMING THE IGNITION (1958–65)

The maker's recommended ignition timing for 1958 and later coil-ignition models should *never* be altered. *The timing is correct if the contact-breaker contacts begin to open with the piston* $\frac{1}{2}$ *in.** *before T.D.C. (top dead centre)*,

* Note the following with regard to pre-1964 350 c.c. Model 16 ("Sceptre") engines after engine number 41575: the contacts should begin to open with the piston $\frac{11}{32}$ in. before T.D.C. with the automatic timing control fully advanced; on pre-1964 350 c.c. engines after engine number 41575 the contacts with the automatic timing control in the fully advanced position. Note that the timing is also correct if the contacts begin to open with the piston $\frac{1}{8}$ in.* before T.D.C., with the automatic timing-control in the fully *retarded* position. The ignition can therefore be re-timed, using one of two methods.

In the event of the automatic timing-control unit being removed from the taper on the inlet camshaft extension, retiming is, of course, necessary. It is also necessary when occasion is had to remove the main cover from the timing case (housing the two camwheels and the engine pinion). The following items are required when retiming the ignition—

(a) A small rod or portion of a stiff wheel spoke (about $5\frac{1}{2}$ in. long).
(b) An automatic timing-control unit withdrawal tool (Part No. 024328).

1. Before Timing the Ignition. Remove: (a) the sparking plug and its h.t. cable; (b) the cover from the off-side of the rocker-box; and (c) the contact-breaker plate and the automatic timing-control unit. Remove the ignition timing-control unit from the inlet camshaft extension as described on page 66. Before removing the plate, on which the contact-breaker and capacitor are assembled, and behind which the ignition timing-control unit is fitted, check that the contact-breaker gap is correct (*see* page 63). This is important because the gap appreciably affects the ignition timing.

2. Identifying Piston Position. Rotate the engine *forwards* slowly until the piston is at or near top dead centre on the compression stroke (inlet valve opens and then closes), with both valves fully closed. Engage fourth gear and insert the timing rod or portion of spoke through the sparking-plug hole. Then rock the engine gently backwards and forwards until *no movement* is felt on the rod which should be held as vertically as possible. When the rod remains dead still, with both valves fully closed, the piston is at the extreme top of its stroke, i.e. in the top dead centre (T.D.C.) position.

Scratch a mark on the timing rod flush with the top face of the sparking-plug hole, and remove the rod. Then scratch another mark $\frac{1}{2}$ in. or $\frac{1}{8}$ in.* *above* the T.D.C. mark, according to whether you decide to retime with the automatic ignition timing-control fully advanced or fully retarded respectively.

3. Timing the Ignition. With the piston at true T.D.C., fit the automatic ignition timing-control unit to the inlet camshaft extension, with the gap formed by the two bob weights (*see* Fig. 32) in line with the two tapped

---

should begin to open with the piston $\frac{3}{16}$ in. before T.D.C. when the A.T.C. is fully retarded. On 1964–5 350 and 500 c.c. engines the contacts should begin to open 8·9 mm. (34 degrees) and 10·98 mm. (38 degrees) before T.D.C. respectively with the automatic timing control fully advanced.

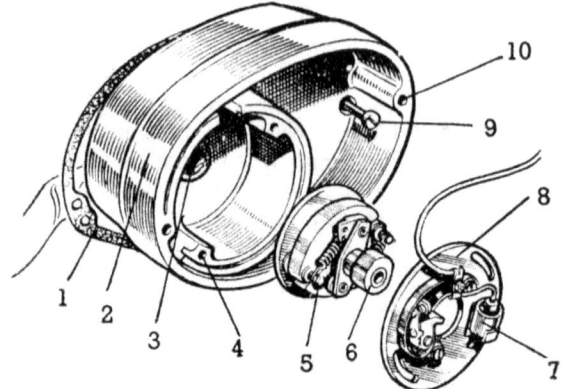

Fig. 31. The Timing Case Main Cover, Automatic Ignition Timing-control Unit and Contact-breaker Plate Shown Removed

1. Washer (between engine timing case and 2).
2. Timing-case main cover.
3. Bush for inlet camshaft extension.
4. Hole (one of two) for screws securing 8.
5. Automatic ignition timing-control unit.
6. Cam (operating contact-breaker).
7. Capacitor.
8. Contact-breaker plate with elongated holes for timing.
9. Screw (one of five) securing 2 to timing case.
10. Hole (one of two) for screws securing timing-case outer cover.

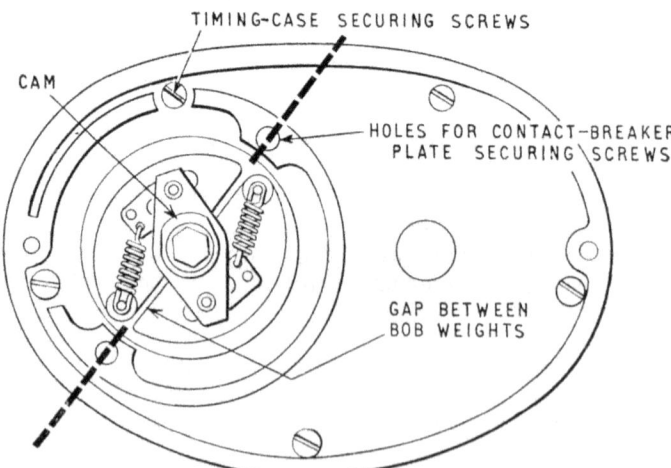

Fig. 32. Correct Alignment when Fitting the Automatic Ignition Timing-control Unit

Note the cam position and the dotted alignment line.

GENERAL MAINTENANCE

holes for the contact-breaker plate securing-screws (shown at 4 in Fig. 31). When correctly positioned the peak of the cam (i.e. its narrowest part) is approximately at 12 o'clock. Press the ignition timing-control unit firmly on to the tapered camshaft extension and deliver a sharp tap on the cam before replacing and tightening the central securing bolt. If the *fully advanced* method of timing is to be used, insert a wooden wedge between the bob weights to fully separate them.

Replace the marked timing rod through the sparking-plug hole, and with fourth gear still engaged, turn the engine slowly *backwards* until the *highest* of the two marks scratched on the rod is flush with the top face of the sparking-plug hole. Position the contact-breaker plate in its housing (*see* Fig. 31) with the capacitor at 3 o'clock and *lightly* tighten the two screws securing the contact-breaker plate.

To determine the exact moment when the contacts commence to open, insert a thin cellophane slip between the contacts and exert a gentle pull on the slip when the contact-breaker plate is moved slowly in a *clockwise* direction. When the correct plate position for contact opening is obtained, tighten the two contact-breaker plate securing-screws (if using the fully *retarded* method of ignition timing).

If a wooden wedge is used to *fully advance* the ignition timing, scribe a pencil line on the contact-breaker plate, and a similar line on the plate housing, with both lines in register. Withdraw the contact-breaker plate, remove the wedge, replace the contact-breaker plate with the two scribed lines in register. Afterwards fully tighten the two contact-breaker plate securing-screws. Before replacing the sparking plug, h.t. lead, and rocker-box cover, again check the ignition timing.

TAPPET ADJUSTMENT

Check and, if necessary, rectify the tappet adjustment every 3,000 miles. It is generally necessary to adjust both tappets after every 5,000 miles. The adjustment must always be checked after decarbonizing the engine and grinding-in the valves. The need for tappet adjustment more frequently than about once every 5,000 miles is generally due to some fault which should be investigated. It is of vital importance to keep the adjustment correct to prevent damage to the valves and to maintain high engine performance.

The Clearance. On 350 c.c. 500 c.c. models the correct tappet clearance is *nil* with both valves closed and the engine *cold* (warm, not hot, on all 1955–7 models). A clearance of *nil* implies that the push-rods are free to rotate without any appreciable up-and-down play.

Detach the cover from the off-side of the rocker-box after removing the three retaining nuts and fibre washers. This exposes the inlet and exhaust tappet adjustment. As may be seen in Fig. 33, each push-rod has a cupped adjustable head *A* secured by a lock-nut *B* to the push-rod sleeve *C*.*

Adjusting the Tappets (1955 Onwards). Turn the engine (350 c.c. or 500 c.c.) over slowly until the piston is at T.D.C. on the compression stroke, with both valves closed. See that the exhaust-valve lifter is not preventing the exhaust valve from seating fully. Then check the tappet clearance for both tappets (*see* above). Referring to Fig. 33, if an adjustment of either or both tappets is required, hold the push-rod sleeve *C* with one spanner, and with another loosen the lock-nut *B*. Then screw the adjustable head *A* up or down until a tappet clearance of *nil* is obtained. Afterwards tighten the lock-nut (*B*) (without moving head (*A*)) and again check the clearance.

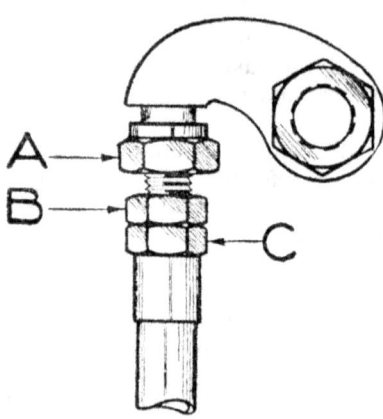

FIG. 33. TAPPET ADJUSTMENT ON 350 C.C., 500 C.C. O.H.V. ENGINES
(*see also* Fig. 34)

After Tappet Adjustment. Turn the engine over until both valves are closed. Check that the push-rods are free to rotate without appreciable up-and-down movement. Fit the cover to the off-side of the rocker-box and replace the three retaining nuts. Make sure that the three fibre washers are also replaced beneath the nuts. When tightening the nuts avoid using excessive pressure on the spanner. Such pressure is quite unnecessary, because a rubber fillet is incorporated at the rocker-box cover joint. Moderate pressure with the spanner will suffice to prevent oil leakage. Tighten the three nuts evenly.

DECARBONIZING AND VALVE GRINDING

The exact time at which the removal of carbon deposits becomes necessary depends to some extent on (*a*) quality of the fuel used and (*b*) the driving conditions. Under normal circumstances it is advisable to remove the cylinder head, decarbonize and, *if necessary*, grind-in the valves *when* the performance declines. If the engine develops a tendency to "knock" when accelerating quickly or hill-climbing, power declines and fuel consumption increases, this confirms that the time for decarbonizing is due.

* Note that a new sleeve cannot be fitted to an existing light-alloy push-rod, the sleeve and the rod being simultaneously threaded (internally) for the adjustable head, during manufacture.

Do *not* remove the cylinder barrel unless you have *good* reason to inspect the piston and rings, and perhaps the bore of the cylinder. Remove the barrel, however, if any stiffness of the piston occurs, or if loss of compression (not caused by bad valve seating) develops. Decarbonizing and grinding-in the valves is quite simple if you follow the correct procedure (Sections 1–22).

1. Remove Petrol Tank. It is necessary to remove the petrol tank before detaching the rocker-box and cylinder head prior to decarbonizing, also when undertaking any major engine overhaul work.

To remove the petrol tank on 1955–9 models first close both petrol taps and remove the cap nut which secures each petrol pipe banjo connector. Use one spanner to hold the tap and another spanner to unscrew the cap nut. Be careful not to lose the four fibre washers, fitted one on each side of each banjo connexion. Sever the wires which interlace the four tank-fixing bolts. Then remove the bolts and withdraw the tank. Note the layout (*see* Fig. 39) of the various rubber and metal washers and tubular sleeves to ensure correct replacement.

To remove the petrol tank on 1960–1 models first turn off the petrol and disconnect both petrol pipes, release the dualseat front fixing bolts, and raise the dualseat slightly. Now remove the two fixing bolts securing the front end of the tank (*see* Fig. 39) and also remove the rear fixing bolt. Then remove the petrol tank.

To remove the petrol tank on 1962–5 models first turn off the petrol and disconnect both petrol pipes. The tank is secured by two nuts at the front end (*see* Fig. 40) and also by a rubber ring encircling the frame tube and anchored on two tank projections. A rubber block is provided between the bottom of the tank and the frame tube. Remove the two self-locking nuts on each of the two front tank-mountings. Then depress or pull back the "nose" of the dualseat, lift off the rubber band from its anchorage, and withdraw the tank.

2. Remove Rocker-box (1955–65). After tank removal, the next step towards cylinder-head removal is to take off the rocker-box and push-rods. First remove the three nuts retaining the cover to the off-side of the rocker-box. Also remove the three fibre washers beneath the nuts. Then take off the rocker-box end-cover as shown in Fig. 34. Disconnect the upper union of the oil-feed pipe to the rocker-box. Now rotate the engine slowly until both inlet and exhaust valves are closed. Detach the engine-steady bracket (*see* Fig. 34) between the rocker-box and frame top-tube. To do this, remove the nuts and washers from the rocker-box bolt extensions and also the bolt from the frame clip.

With a spanner, remove the nine bolts securing the rocker-box to the cylinder head. Disconnect the exhaust-valve lifter cable. Grip the rocker-box, tilt up its right-hand side and withdraw both push-rods. These should not be interchanged, and for this reason should be marked or placed so that they can subsequently be identified. Now carefully lift the rocker-box clear of the cylinder head.

FIG. 34. PREPARING FOR ROCKER-BOX REMOVAL

The petrol tank, the oil-feed pipe to the rocker-box, and the rocker-box cover have been removed. The next operation is to remove the engine-steady bracket connecting the rocker-box to the frame top-tube, and then remove the rocker-box securing bolts.

3. Remove Cylinder Head. Having removed the fuel tank and rocker-box as previously described, unscrew the sparking plug.* Then proceed to remove, or partially remove, the exhaust system.

To remove the exhaust system, first remove the nuts and washers which secure the exhaust pipe and silencer to their stays. Then pull the exhaust pipe and silencer away from the stays, and pull the pipe downwards from the port in the cylinder head.

Remove the Amal carburettor by disconnecting the air filter (where fitted) and removing the two nuts securing the carburettor flange to the

* Should the sparking plug be difficult to unscrew, do not apply excessive force with the box spanner. Brush some paraffin or penetrating oil round the plug body and allow to soak prior to further use of the spanner.

cylinder head. The carburettor may be allowed to rest on the saddle or on the platform above the dynamo (1955-7), as shown in Fig. 36; it is not necessary to remove the throttle and air slides from the carburettor.

Next remove the four bolts which retain the cylinder head to the cylinder barrel. If these are stiff, brush paraffin round their heads and allow to penetrate before again using the spanner. Lift the cylinder head from the cylinder barrel and simultaneously remove the push-rod cover tubes (1955-63) which come away with the cylinder head.

4. To Remove Cylinder Barrel. Rotate the engine so that the piston is near B.D.C. Next remove the four nuts which secure the cylinder barrel to the crankcase, and then gently draw the barrel off the piston. Steady the latter with one hand as the barrel is withdrawn, and take great care not to allow the piston to fall sharply against the connecting rod. After removing the cylinder barrel, cover the mouth of the crankcase with a clean rag.

5. Piston Removal. To remove the fully-floating gudgeon-pin, it is only necessary to extract *one* circlip with the snipe-nosed pliers provided in the tool kit. Push the gudgeon-pin out from the opposite side and remove the piston. The gudgeon-pin is an easy sliding fit in the piston bosses and the small-end bush. If the piston is not of the split-skirt type, scratch an "F" on the inside to indicate which is the front. Mark the pin also.

Condition of Piston. A piston will run well for very many thousands of miles; but eventually loss of compression and/or piston slap occurs due to wear of the piston, rings, and cylinder bore, especially the last-mentioned. Examine the cylinder bore occasionally for longitudinal scores and circumferential ridges. Also inspect the piston for blackening of the skirt, scores, smearing, and other possible damage, particularly near the ring lands.

Cylinder Rebores. After a very considerable mileage (when wear at the top of the bore reaches 0·008 in.) it is usually essential to have a rebore and fit an oversize piston and rings to restore the compression and performance of the engine to normal. The makers provide for rebores 0·020 in. and 0·040 oversize, and can supply 0·020 in. and 0·040 in. oversize pistons and rings to suit. Running-in is, of course, necessary after a rebore.

6. Removing Piston Rings. The piston rings should not be disturbed if their condition is good, they are free in their grooves, and engine compression remains good. The rings can be removed by "peeling off" with a small knife, but it is preferable to remove them with the aid of three strips of thin sheet-metal (about ¼ in. wide) inserted beneath each ring as shown in Fig. 35. The rings, being made of cast iron, cannot safely be sprung out wider than the piston-crown diameter. If the rings are stuck with carbon, apply some paraffin. If this fails, use a proprietary ring-removal tool.

7. **Examining Piston Rings.** Inspect the two compression rings and the scraper ring very carefully. To ensure good engine compression the piston rings must have good springiness, be free, but not slack in their grooves, have a polished surface all round, and have their gaps equally spaced and of the correct size. If inspection reveals that the ring surfaces are bright all round, they are obviously making good circumferential contact with the cylinder bore and can be regarded as serviceable. If, on the other hand, the surfaces are discoloured or scorched at some points, contact is poor and it is desirable to reject the rings and fit new ones. The same applies where the rings are vertically slack in their grooves.

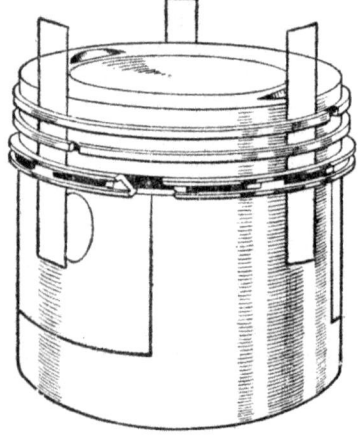

Fig. 35. The Safest Method of Removing and Fitting Piston Rings

Clean the rings thoroughly on their inside faces, also the ends of the rings, and the slots in the scraper ring (see Fig. 35). Piston rings are made to very precise dimensions, and it is not generally practicable to fit oversize rings unless the piston is renewed also. Always fit genuine A.J.S. rings which are dimensionally correct. To reduce cylinder-bore wear, a chromium-plated top compression ring is fitted to 1955 and later 350 and 500 c.c. engines.

8. **Piston Ring Dimensions.** The widths of the compression rings and the slotted scraper ring on all engines are $\frac{1}{16}$ in. and $\frac{1}{8}$ in. respectively. The normal ring gap is 0·006 in. and rings should be renewed when the gap exceeds 0·030 in. The normal clearance of each ring in its groove is 0·003 in. (0·002 in. on 1955–65 engines).

After a considerable mileage, or if loss of compression occurs with the valves in good condition, check the gap of each piston ring. The best method of checking the gap is to push the ring squarely into the bore of the cylinder barrel with the aid of the piston and then check the gap between the ends of the ring with a feeler gauge. If the gap proves excessive, fit new A.J.S. rings (already gapped); if the gap is insufficient, remove some metal from *one* end of the ring to increase the gap to 0·006 in.

9. **To Remove Valves (1955 Onwards).** On all 1955 and later engines a modified and improved hairpin valve-spring assembly renders it unnecessary

to employ a valve-spring compressor to remove the valves though a compressor (see Fig. 37) is needed for replacing them. To remove each hairpin valve spring, insert a finger in the spring coil and pull the coil sharply upward. You can then take off the valve-spring collar and split collet, and withdraw the valve. If the tapered split collet is stuck, deliver a sharp tap on the collar to free it.

Note that the modified seat for the valve spring has a raised impression on its under-side; this registers with a hole drilled in the valve-guide boss

FIG. 36. SCRAPING THE CARBON OFF THE PISTON WITH A BLUNT SCREWDRIVER
The piston should first be positioned at T.D.C. When chipping off the carbon, hold the screwdriver in the manner shown.

to ensure proper location. Note also that, as hitherto, the valves are not interchangeable and must be identified for correct replacement.

10. Removing Carbon Deposits. The best tool to use for scraping off the carbon deposits is an old (blunted) screwdriver, or a proprietary scraper (obtainable from most accessory dealers). For cleaning piston-ring grooves a suitable scraper can be made up by fitting a handle to a piece of broken piston-ring, or better still a proprietary tool can be obtained for the purpose. It is worth while decarbonizing *thoroughly*, as carbon deposits form less rapidly on smooth surfaces. Where head deposits are found to be very hard, the application of paraffin will facilitate their removal.

If the cylinder barrel has not been removed, scrape off all carbon from the piston crown, but *on no account use any abrasive*. Should this get between the piston and cylinder (as it probably would) your A.J.S. would rapidly go into a decline! Be very careful not to make any deep scratch marks on the comparatively soft surface of the light-alloy piston. Scrape off all carbon from the inside of the combustion chamber. Do not forget to chip off and completely remove all carbon from the valve ports,* the vicinity of the valves, the valve heads, and the sparking-plug hole. It is permissible to use some *fine* emery cloth to polish up a cast-iron combustion chamber, but if this is done the cylinder head must afterwards be very thoroughly cleaned and all trace of abrasive particles removed. Use a rag damped with paraffin. Do not touch the cylinder bore.

If the cylinder barrel *and* piston have been removed, it may be advisable to scrape carbon off the inside of the piston but, unless the deposits are thick, this should not be done. Remove all carbon from the piston crown, but *do not touch the skirt*. Any attempt to scrape the piston skirt may have disastrous results. The piston-ring grooves, sometimes need attention. Clean these up thoroughly, but be very careful not to damage the actual metal comprising the sides of the grooves. Make sure that the holes in the groove for the scraper ring (*see* Fig. 35) are unobstructed. The cleaning of piston rings is referred to on page 76. After decarbonizing is complete, clean all parts thoroughly with suitable clean rags and paraffin.

11. Grinding-in the Valves. Although the engine manufacturers recommend that the valves be inspected every time the engine is decarbonized, it should be understood that excessive valve grinding is not advisable as this is liable to cause the valves to become "pocketed," with a resultant loss of engine efficiency. If the valves *are* seating perfectly, leave them alone; otherwise grind-in both valves.

After removing the valves for grinding-in, clean both valve heads thoroughly and polish the valve stems with some worn *fine* emery cloth, using an up-and-down motion with the emery cloth held between the forefinger and thumb. Then proceed to grind-in each valve as described below, using a good grinding paste such as Richford's (tins contain two grades, coarse and fine).

To grind-in a valve, first smear the bevelled face of the valve with a *thin* layer of grinding paste. If the valve face and seat are only slightly pitted, it should be sufficient to use a *fine* grade of paste only. Serious pitting may necessitate the preliminary application of a coarse grade and, if the pitting is very severe, it may be necessary to have the valve seats refaced at a garage with a cutter having a cutting angle of 45 degrees.

Insert the valve in its seat and oscillate the valve about a quarter of a turn backwards and forwards by means of a suitable valve holder. Maintain a slight pressure between the valve and its seat and lift the valve

---

* If close inspection reveals any roughness of the metal surfaces inside the inlet or exhaust port, it is beneficial to smooth out such irregularities with a curved rifler.

occasionally (when the abrasive ceases to bite) and turn it to a new position. Continue to grind-in the valve until a continuous matt ring is present on both the valve seat and the valve. Generally one application of grinding paste is sufficient for the inlet valve, but the exhaust valve may require several applications to obtain good results. The part number of the A.J.S. valve holder is 017482. A proprietary suction-rubber type is also suitable.

12. After Grinding-in. See that every trace of grinding paste is eradicated by cleaning the valves and the two seats with petrol and a clean rag. To ensure that the valve guides are free from damaging abrasive, it is advisable to draw a piece of clean rag through both guides.

13. To Check Valve Spring Length (1955–65). After much use the hard-pressed valve springs may weaken under the influence of heat, and thereby spoil the quick and positive action of the valves, which is so vital to high engine efficiency. The condition of the valve springs is reflected in their free length, which should be checked very occasionally with a small rule.

All 1955–65 single-cylinder O.H.V. engines have hairpin instead of coil-type valve-springs. Renew any hairpin valve spring whose free length is $\frac{3}{16}$ in.–$\frac{1}{4}$ in. less than its normal free length: 2 in. (between the centre of wire).

Removing and Replacing Valve Guides. Before removing an inlet valve guide clean thoroughly its protruding end. Then apply gentle heat and press the valve guide downwards. To remove an exhaust valve guide apply gentle heat, press the guide upwards sufficiently to allow removal of the external circlip. Then clean the top of the valve guide and press downwards to remove it. When replacing the valve guides re-heat them and see that the valve guide projection (the top of the guide to the boss) is $\frac{1}{2}$ in. This applies to both valve guides. In the case of both valve guides make sure that the oil hole in the guide is in correct alignment.

To Replace Valves (1955 Onwards). Thoroughly clean the bores of both valve guides and smear a film of engine oil on the stems of the valves. Replace the latter in their correct guides. On the 350 c.c. engine the inlet valve can immediately be recognized, as it has a head of larger diameter than the exhaust valve. On the 500 c.c. engine, however, the dimensions of both valves are identical, though the material differs. In this case, before fitting the valves, note the markings "IN" and "EX" on top of the inlet- and exhaust-valve stems respectively, above the grooves for the split collets. Insert suitable packing beneath each valve head and place the cylinder head in its normal position on the bench. Then fit each hairpin valve spring as follows.

Fit the valve-spring top collar and the split collet.* Then position the hairpin valve springs and proceed to compress each spring with the special A.J.S. valve-spring compressor shown in Fig. 37. The standard tool kit does not include this compressor, but it can be obtained from the makers or an A.J.S. dealer. To use the compressor, apply the upper end of

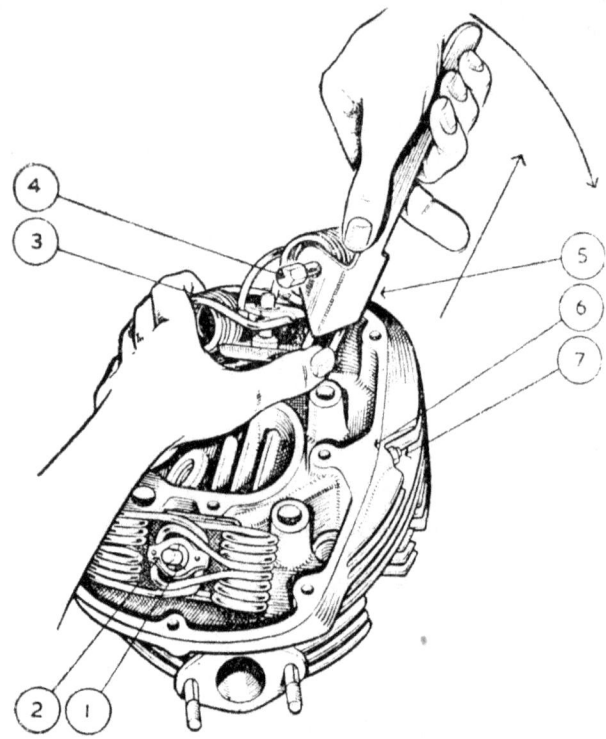

FIG. 37. VALVE-SPRING COMPRESSOR (PART NO. 018276) FOR ENGINES WITH HAIRPIN VALVE SPRINGS (1955 ONWARDS)

KEY TO FIG. 37

1. Split collet.
2. Valve-spring collar.
3. Valve-spring collar.
4. Rocker-box bolt.
5. Valve-spring compressor.
6. Oil duct from rocker-box to inlet valve guide.
7. Screw controlling oil feed to inlet-valve stem.

the valve spring to the groove in the top cap; insert a short rod (e.g. a rocker-box securing bolt) through the holes in the compressor (and the valve-spring coils) and pull upward and outward until the ends of the

* Make quite sure that the two machined grooves on the bore of the split collet register with the corresponding rings on the valve stem.

GENERAL MAINTENANCE

spring prong can be rested on the seat. Then with the fingers, press down.

Remove the rod (or rocker-box bolt) as soon as the compressor lies against the cylinder head, but maintain finger pressure until you have removed the rod (or bolt) and the compressor tool. Finally push the spring down until it locates properly. Its prong ends must lie flat on the seat.

15. Fitting Piston Rings. If these have been removed, fit them in their grooves, which should first be oiled. The safest method of fitting the piston rings is to use three strips of thin sheet-metal, as illustrated in Fig. 35. Fit the (bottom) scraper ring first, and then the two compression rings. Space the ring gaps evenly, that is, at 120 degrees to each other. It is assumed that the ring gaps are within the permissible limits (*see* page 76). If new rings are fitted, these are correctly gapped by the makers and are ready for immediate use.

On 1955 and all subsequent engines the top compression ring is chromium plated and one edge is marked TOP. See that this ring is replaced accordingly. Note that after a considerable mileage the word TOP may become unreadable, but for a very considerable period the correct assembly position for the chromium-plated ring can be determined by the extra brightness of the edge which makes contact with the cylinder bore. The bright edge must be at the *bottom*. When eventually the ring becomes bright over its full width (indicating full contact with the bore), it is permissible to replace the top compression ring either way round.

16. Replacing Piston. It is assumed that all parts are thoroughly clean and that the piston rings have been refitted. Smear some engine oil on the gudgeon-pin and then offer up the piston to the small-end of the connecting-rod. The piston must be replaced in *exactly* the same position as before. If it is of the split-skirt type, the split itself must face to the *front* of the machine. This is essential.

Next insert the gudgeon-pin from the side from which the circlip has been removed. Centralize the gudgeon-pin, and with the small snipe-nosed pliers in the tool kit replace the circlip, using a rotary movement to ensure that it beds snugly into its groove. Perfect fitting of the circlip is essential to prevent damage. If the condition of the old circlip is suspect, renew the circlip immediately.

17. To Replace Cylinder Barrel. A *new* washer must be fitted to the crankcase, and its cylinder barrel side should be coated with liquid jointing-compound. Make sure that none of the compound chokes any of the oil holes and that the holes register properly. Now smear some engine oil on the piston and cylinder bore, and then turn the engine so that the piston is at or near B.D.C. Verify that the piston-ring gaps are spaced at 120 degrees and remove the rag from the mouth of the crankcase.

Ease the cylinder barrel carefully over the piston, compressing each ring as it enters the bore mouth, to enable the barrel to slide over the piston without friction. Finally replace the four cylinder-barrel retaining nuts. Tighten the four nuts, first finger-tight, and then firmly in a diagonal order, turning each nut about one-quarter of a turn at a time.

18. Fit the Cylinder Head. Wipe the bottom face of the cylinder head and the top edge of the cylinder barrel clean. Then fit (1955–63) the push-

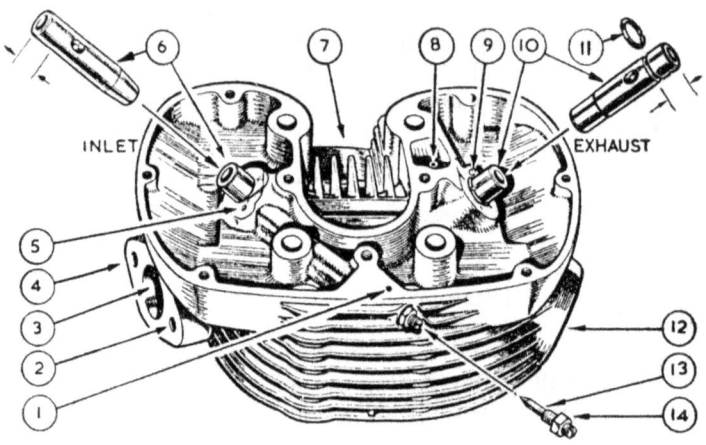

Fig. 38. Showing Details of A.J.S. Cylinder Head
Both valve guides and the needle adjusting screw for the oil feed to the inlet valve stem are shown withdrawn.

KEY TO FIG. 38

1. Hole for oil feed to inlet valve.
2. Tapped hole for carburettor securing stud.
3. Inlet port.
4. Tapped hole for carburettor securing stud.
5. Hole for dowel locating valve spring seat.
6. Inlet valve guide.
7. Threaded hole for sparking plug.
8. Hole for oil feed to exhaust valve.
9. Hole for dowel pin locating valve spring seat.
10. Exhaust valve guide.
11. Circlip for valve guide.
12. Exhaust port.
13. Needle adjusting screw for oil feed to inlet valve.
14. Lock-nut for 13.

rod cover tubes to the cylinder head. See that the rubber gaskets are in good condition, and fitted between the top ends of the cover tubes and cylinder head. If the push-rod cover tubes were pulled away from the cylinder head during stripping down, it would probably be found that the rubber gaskets have remained located in the cylinder head. Also check that the metal washers are interposed between the top edges of the rubber gaskets and the recesses in the cylinder head.

GENERAL MAINTENANCE

Fit the cylinder head gasket on the top edge of the cylinder barrel. If the gasket is not in perfect condition, renew it. Whether you fit a new gasket or use the old one, it is advisable to anneal it just before placing it on the cylinder barrel. To anneal the gasket, heat it to a "blood red" colour and plunge into cold clean water. Place the two rubber glands round the inlet and exhaust tappet guides. Then replace the cylinder head on the barrel, complete with push-rod cover tubes (1955–63), and fit the four cylinder head bolts. Each bolt must be fitted with a plain steel-washer. Tighten each bolt a few turns and then gradually tighten all four, using a diagonal sequence to ensure an even pressure being exerted on the cylinder head.

19. Fit the Rocker-box (1955 Onwards). Clean the lower face of the rocker-box and the upper face of the cylinder head. Next slowly turn the engine until the piston is at T.D.C. with both tappets right down. Inspect the cylinder-head composition washer (renew if not perfect), and lay the washer on the cylinder head.

Position the rocker-box and then raise slightly the off-side of the box to permit the two long push-rods to be inserted in their original positions. Now fit the *nine* rocker-box securing bolts. Note that the bolt with the short head goes in the centre right-hand position, while the bolts having the threaded extensions go one on each side of the central short-headed bolt. Tighten in a diagonal order and evenly all nine rocker-box securing bolts.

Fit the engine steady-stay and then rotate the engine a few times so as to be sure that the various parts bed right down. Now reconnect the exhaust-valve lifter control and check the tappet clearances (*see* page 71).

20. Fit Oil Pipe and Rocker-box Cover. Reconnect the oil-feed pipe from the pump to the rocker-box.* Use two spanners when tightening the upper union, to prevent the union (screwed into the rocker-box) from turning. Fit a new rubber fillet to the rocker-box side cover if examination of the fillet shows deterioration. Then fit the rocker-box side cover to the rocker-box, and replace the three fibre washers and securing nuts. Tighten these nuts evenly, but not too tightly. The provision of a rubber fillet renders excessive tightening quite unnecessary.

21. Final Engine Assembly. Final reassembly, after decarbonizing, is completed by replacing the Amal carburettor, the sparking plug, and exhaust system. When fitting the Amal carburettor, it is important to obtain an absolutely airtight joint at the attachment flange. Renew the washer if not perfect, also the copper washer for the sparking plug. Smear some graphite paste on the plug threads.

* This applies to 1955–63 models. 1964–5 models have a by-pass from the main oil feed, taken from the timing-case cover.

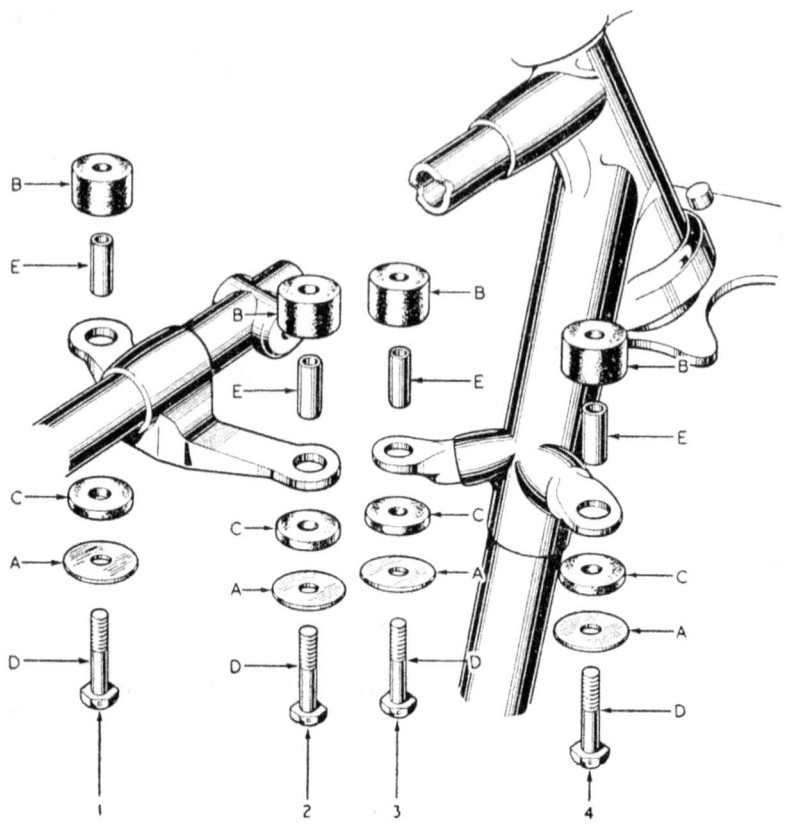

Fig. 39. Petrol-tank Mounting (1955–9)

With the arrangement shown, which includes four sleeves, the tank-fixing bolts can and must be fully tightened on assembly. On the 1960–1 models two bolts secure the front of the tank, and one bolt the rear.

KEY TO FIG. 39

A. Metal washer.
B. Thick rubber pad.
C. Thin rubber pad.
D. Petrol tank-fixing bolt.
E. Metal sleeve for fixing bolt D.

22. Replace Petrol Tank (1955–9). The arrangement of the tank-fixing bolts and washers on all 1955–9 models is shown in Fig. 39. As may be seen, an identical arrangement is provided for each of the four mounting brackets. Metal sleeves (*shown* at (E)) are included to enable the fixing bolts to be *fully* tightened without over-compressing the rubber pads. To replace the petrol tank, proceed as follows—

(1) Insert one of the four sleeves (E) in each of the four thick rubber pads (B), so that the top of the sleeve is flush with the top of the pad.

GENERAL MAINTENANCE

(2) Lay the four thick rubber pads (*B*) on the ends of the four petrol-tank support-brackets, complete with sleeves (*E*) protruding through the bracket holes.

(3) Correctly position the petrol tank.

(4) Slide one of the four metal washers (*A*) over each of the four tank-fixing bolts (*D*). Afterwards slip a thin rubber pad (*C*) over each tank-fixing bolt.

(5) Insert all four tank-fixing bolts, complete with rubber pads and metal washers.

(6) Tighten *firmly* the four tank-fixing bolts.

(7) Interlace the four tank-fixing bolts in pairs, using 22 gauge copper wire.

(8) Reconnect both petrol pipes, and with a spanner hold the taps when firmly tightening the cap-nuts.

Replace Petrol Tank (1960–1). The method of securing the petrol tank is similar to that used on 1955–9 models and shown in Fig. 39 except that *three* instead of four fixing bolts are used, two at the front and one at the rear. The rubber pads, washers, and sleeves are similar and similarly arranged. The 1955–9 instructions therefore apply except in regard to the number of fixing bolt assemblies to be fitted.

Replace Petrol Tank (1962–5). On 1962–5 models the method of securing the petrol tank is quite different (*see* page 73) to the arrangement used on 1955–9 and 1960–1 models. As may be seen in Fig. 40, the forward end of the tank has two tubular holders open at their bottom ends. Position the petrol tank with the two front bolts, long rubber pads and washers located in the holders and pass the mounting bolts through the holes in the two support brackets. Then fit the two washers and nuts underneath and tighten the nuts securely. Also fit the rubber ring and see that it is anchored securely to the projections on the tank. Note that when fitting the petrol tank it is necessary to pull back the "nose" of the dualseat. Finally reconnect the petrol pipes.

VALVE TIMING

The valve timing used on A.J.S. engines is the result of most careful calculation, experiment, and design. Foolish indeed is the motor-cyclist who imagines that he can improve on this setting, which is shown in degrees of crankshaft rotation in Fig. 41.

After dismantling the timing gears it is necessary to re-time the valves, but this does not require actual checking of the timing by attaching a degree disc to the crankshaft and measuring in degrees of crankshaft rotation the exact periods when the inlet valve opens and the exhaust valve

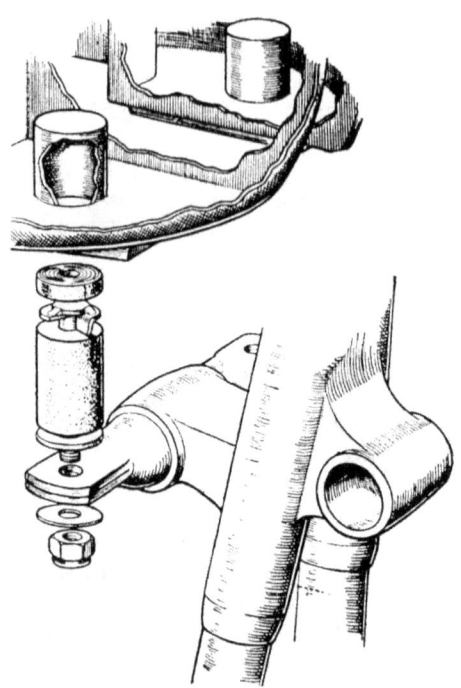

Fig. 40. Mounting of Front End of Petrol Tank (1962–5)

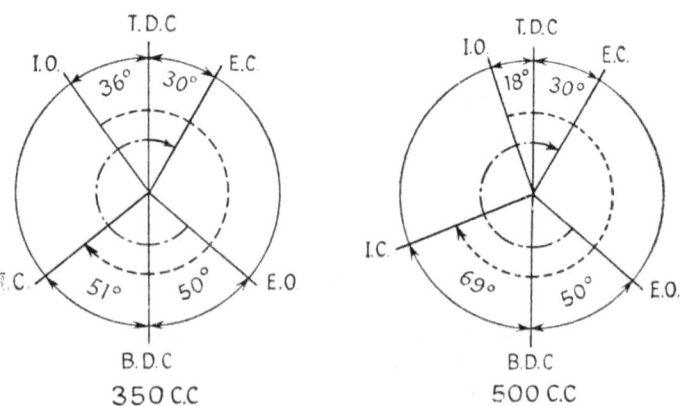

Fig. 41. Valve Timing Diagram for 1955–65 Touring-type Engines

The above timings assume the valves to be 0·001 in. off their seats. When checking the valve timings on all engines, set both tappet clearances at 0·016 in. to ensure that the tappets are well clear of the quietening curves.

closes. The timing gears have a dot system of identification which makes correct replacement of the timing gears a simple operation.

To Dismantle the Timing Gears (1955–7). First remove the foot gear-change pedal to render accessible the timing case. Then remove the cover from the magneto chain-case by unscrewing the six securing screws. Also remove the rocker-box cover after removing the three fixing nuts and fibre washers. Slacken the magneto driving-chain if it is tight.

Unscrew the nut (R.H. thread) that secures the sprocket to the magneto armature-spindle and remove this nut and the washer behind it. With a suitable tool, lever the sprocket off the spindle taper. Should the sprocket be stiff, use a suitable sprocket-drawer. Remove the magneto driving-chain and withdraw the sprocket from the camshaft in the same manner employed to withdraw the other sprocket. The securing nut for this sprocket also has a R.H. thread. Next turn the engine so that *both valves are closed*.

With a screwdriver, remove the five screws that secure the combined magneto chain-case and timing cover to the timing case. The timing gear is then exposed. Before completely removing the timing case cover, hold the two camwheels in position in case they should come adrift when the cover is lifted clear. The two camwheels may then be removed by pulling the camshafts from their bearings.

Generally it is unnecessary to remove the small engine pinion, but if for some reason you decide to extract the pinion, you should undo the nut (L.H. thread) and with a suitable extractor pull the pinion off the crankshaft taper to which it is keyed (one key). To assemble the timing gears, use the procedure for dismantling in the reverse order.

To Dismantle Timing Gears (1958–65). Remove the foot gear-change pedal and then remove the outer cover from the timing case after removing its two securing screws. Next remove the contact-breaker plate and the automatic ignition-control unit as described on page 66. Then remove the five screws which retain the timing-case main cover (*see* Fig. 31) and pull away the cover. This exposes the twin-camwheel timing gear shown in Fig. 43. If the washer (shown at 1 in Fig. 31) is damaged, this must be renewed. While removing the timing-case main cover, hold both camwheels in position in case they should come away during the withdrawal of the cover. Now pull the inlet and exhaust camshafts from their bearings.

The small engine pinion is a taper fit and is keyed on to the timing-side shaft. The mark on the pinion is central with the keyway. Removal of the pinion is rarely required. To remove the pinion undo the retaining nut (L.H. thread) and with a suitable extractor pull the pinion off the tapered timing-side shaft. Use the dismantling procedure in the reverse order for assembling, and re-time the ignition (*see* page 68).

When Fitting Timing Cover (1964–5 Engines). On 1964–5 engines with a gear-type pump it is important to see that the oil seal is under light pressure when fitting the timing cover. The pressure of the oil seal should move the timing cover outwards, making a gap of about 0·010 in. If no pressure exists, fit packing shims between the oil seal and the pump body. Excessive pressure should be avoided as this can mutilate the oil seal and cause leakage.

Re-timing the Valves (1955–65). To ensure that the valve timing is correct, it is necessary to use the following procedure when assembling the timing gears—
(1) Turn the engine slowly until the dot mark on the small engine pinion is in line with the centre of the bush for the inlet camshaft. The bush concerned is the *rear* one.
(2) Fit the inlet camshaft so that the dot mark on the camwheel registers with the dot mark on the small engine pinion.
(3) Turn the engine slowly *forward* until the dot mark on the small engine pinion is in line with the centre of the bush for the exhaust camshaft (the front bush).
(4) Fit the exhaust camshaft so that the dot mark on the camwheel registers with the dot mark on the engine pinion.

If both camwheels are aligned in accordance with the above procedure, the valve timing *must* be correct, provided the timing-gear teeth have not become excessively worn, in which case it is time that the engine and machine are completely overhauled. It is advisable after assembling the timing gears to check that the tappet adjustment (*see* page 70) is correct, as this affects the valve timing to a small extent. Also check the magneto-chain tension (*see* page 66) and magneto timing on 1955–7 engines.

On 1955 Engines. The inlet camwheel has *three* timing dots marked 1, 2, 3; the exhaust camwheel has two dots marked 1 and 2 as shown in Fig. 42.

On 350 c.c. touring engines align the dot marked 3 on the inlet camwheel with the single dot on the engine pinion. On 500 c.c. touring engines align the timing dot marked 2 on the inlet camwheel with the dot on the engine pinion. The dot marked 2 must also always be used for the exhaust camwheel on all 1955 350 c.c. and 500 c.c. engines.

On 1956–65 Engines. After replacing the timing-case cover on coil-ignition models the ignition must be re-timed (*see* page 68) when fitting the automatic ignition-control unit and the contact-breaker plate.

When fitting the inlet camwheel on 1956–63 350 c.c. and 500 c.c. engines align the dot marked 3 or 2 respectively with the dot mark on the engine pinion. When fitting the exhaust camwheel, align the dot marked 1 with the dot on the engine pinion, and disregard dots marked 2, 3 (*see* Fig. 43). 1964–5 camwheels have a single dot mark.

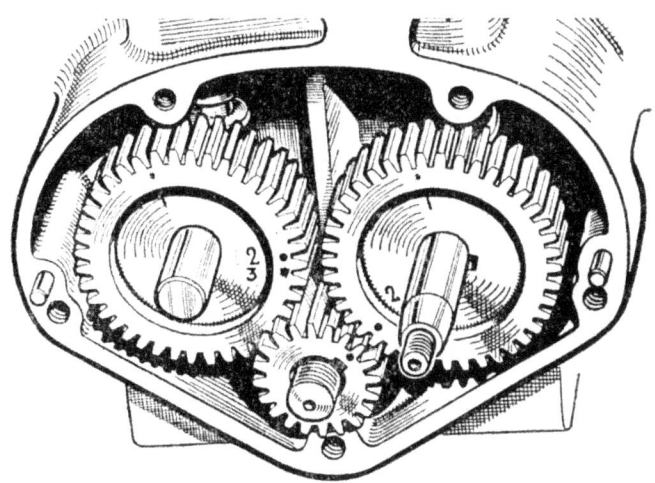

FIG. 42. THE (1955-7) TWIN CAMWHEEL TIMING GEAR WITH 1955 DOT SYSTEM OF TIMING MARKS

Note the following: the nut securing the small engine pinion (which has *one* dot) is shown removed; the inlet camshaft shown has no tapered extension which is provided on 1958-64 coil-ignition models to secure the automatic ignition-control unit.

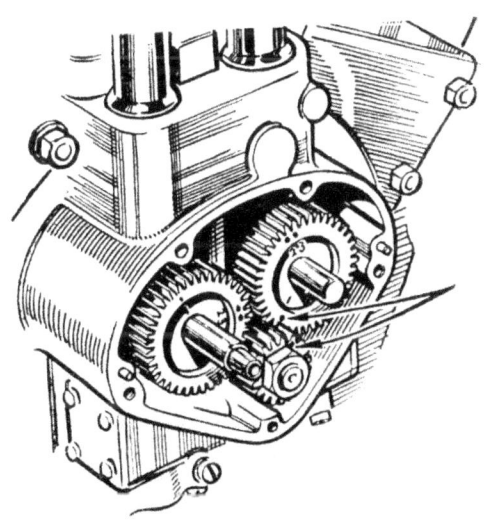

FIG. 43. THE 1958-65 TWIN CAMWHEEL TIMING GEAR WITH 1956-63 DOT SYSTEM OF TIMING MARKS

Note that on all A.J.S. engines the dot mark on the inlet camwheel must always be aligned with the dot on the engine pinion before the exhaust camwheel is dealt with. The arrows show the exhaust camwheel dot marked 1 aligned with the engine pinion dot. The camwheels on all 1964-5 engines have only one dot.

Checking Timing by Degree Method. If for any reason you make an actual check on the valve timing by attaching a degree disc to the crankshaft, it is essential *before* starting to check the timing to adjust both tappet clearances to 0·016 in. with the piston at T.D.C. on the compression stroke.

MOTOR-CYCLE MAINTENANCE

To combine high engine performance with good road performance always pay due regard to the proper maintenance of the lighting system, the brakes, the tyres, and the transmission.

Items Necessary for Maintenance. It is desirable to have the following items available: a can of paraffin, a stiff brush, a tin of *summer-grade* engine oil, a canister of grease (*see* pages 43 and 53), a tin of hydraulic fluid and a flask graduated in fluid oz. (*see* pages 56–7), a tyre-pressure gauge, a Lucas hydrometer and battery filler (*see* Fig. 11), a tyre repair outfit, and a receptacle for draining the gearbox and oil-bath chain case.

For cleaning purposes the following are also needed: some jars or a box, some non-fluffy rags, two chamois leathers, a sponge and pail (if no hose is available), some soft dusters, and a tin of wax or other polish for the enamelled parts.

Tools Required. The A.J.S. tool kit is sufficient for all routine maintenance, stripping down, and assembly, but it is desirable to buy a chain-rivet extractor and a box of spare chain-links. If you are in the mood to tackle repair work as well as maintenance, consider the extra tools suggested on page 59.

The Lighting System. Keep the lights bright by attending to lamp, battery, and (1955–7) dynamo maintenance as described in Chapter III.

Lubrication of Motor-cycle. This is fully explained in Chapter IV. Attend to the lubrication points indicated at 5 to 17 in the Lubrication Chart on page 50.

Keeping Machine Clean. If the enamelled and chromium-plated parts are neglected, the machine will soon become shabby-looking, and serious rusting may occur. On no account leave your A.J.S. soaking wet overnight. If you have not time for thorough cleaning in wet weather, grease the machine all over before using it. When cleaning the machine, use a stiff brush and paraffin for removing filth from the lower part of the gearbox.

The Enamelled Parts. Never try to remove caked mud by attempting to brush or rub it off when dry. Instead, carefully soak it off by means of a

GENERAL MAINTENANCE

hose. When doing this, be careful not to direct the stream of water on to vital and vulnerable components such as a carburettor, dynamo, or magneto. If no hose is available, soak off the mud with a pail of water and a sponge. After removing all mud and dirt, dry the enamelled parts with a chamois leather, and afterwards polish the surfaces with soft dusters and a proprietary wax or other polish.

Cleaning Chromium. On no account use ordinary liquid metal-polish or paste to clean any of the chromium-plated parts. Such cleaners generally contain oleic acid which attacks the chromium. It is permissible, however, to clean the surfaces occasionally with some special chromium-cleaning compound. To remove tarnish (salt deposits), it is advisable to clean the surfaces regularly with a damp chamois leather and afterwards polish them with a soft duster.

To Reduce Tarnishing in Winter. It is a good plan to apply with a soft cloth to all chromium-plated surfaces one or other of the preparations on the market that help to render chromium-plate impervious to moisture—and so reduce tarnishing.

A.J.S. Motor Cycles recommend using "Tekall," obtainable in $\frac{1}{2}$ pt. and 1 pt. tins at most garages and from the A.J.S. spares dept. in $\frac{1}{2}$ pt. tins. A soft rag soaked in "Tekall" should be wiped over the chromium-plated parts. This will leave an almost invisible film which is impervious to moisture.

Nuts and Bolts. Occasionally (about every 3,000 miles) check over all external nuts and bolts for tightness (see page 60). Pay special attention to all drain plugs, the nuts securing the exhaust system, all control-lever clip bolts, the wheel-spindle nuts, the nuts at the base of the fork sliders, the brake-cam spindle nuts, the footrest-hanger nuts, the screws securing the handlebars, the mudguard-securing nuts, and the small screw securing the headlamp front. Also keep a watchful eye on the rear chain spring-link, and the caps for the tyre-inflation valves.

TYRE PRESSURES, WHEEL ALIGNMENT

Tyre Inflation Pressures. Even the best quality rubber is not entirely impervious to air leakage, and tyre-inflation pressures slowly but surely decline in spite of the fact that the tyres and valves are in perfect condition. Therefore check the inflation pressures of both tyres *weekly*, not by "thumbing" the covers or kicking them, but by using a suitable pressure gauge such as the Dunlop pencil-type No. 6, the Schrader No. 7750, the Romac, or the Holdtite. By maintaining the inflation pressures correct, tyre deflation is reduced to the minimum, and maximum comfort, tyre life, and freedom from skidding are assured. Avoid fierce braking and excessive acceleration. Also keep oil off the treads, and maintain the wheels in true alignment.

Correct Pressures. If you ride solo and are of normal weight, you should maintain the inflation pressures of the front and rear tyres at 18 lb. per sq. in. and 22 lb. per sq. in., respectively. If you are not of normal weight

MINIMUM TYRE INFLATION PRESSURES
(Showing load per tyre and recommended pressure in lb. per sq. in.)

Load	Pressure	Load	Pressure
200 lb.	16 lb.	350 lb.	24 lb.
240 lb.	18 lb.	400 lb.	28 lb.
280 lb.	20 lb.	440 lb.	32 lb.

carry heavy equipment, or a pillion passenger, it is necessary to adjust the inflation pressures accordingly. Above are tabulated the correct minimum inflation pressures for specified loads per tyre.

The most satisfactory method of determining the correct inflation pressures required is to ride or take the machine to the nearest weighbridge and check individually the fully-laden weight on the front and rear tyres. Then consult the above table for the front and rear correct minimum inflation pressures. A suitable weighbridge is to be found at most large railway stations and other transport depots. The rider and pillion rider (if carried) must, of course, be seated.

Wheel Alignment (Solo). To check the alignment on a solo A.J.S., a straight-edge or a plain board (with one edge planed perfectly straight and square) about 5 ft. long is required. Alternatively use a taut piece of string tied to an anchorage post.

Jack up the A.J.S. on its stand, with the front and rear wheels parallel to each other. Then check the wheel alignment by holding the straight-edge, board, or string in contact with both tyres (about 4 in. above the ground and parallel with it). It should contact the front and rear of each tyre if the wheels are correctly aligned. This applies, of course, only to models having identical-section front and rear tyres. Where a front tyre of smaller section is fitted, check that the gaps between the straight-edge (or string) and the tyre sides are equal, front and rear. If the wheels are out of alignment, rectify matters by means of the adjusters screwed into the rear-fork ends (*see* pages 101–2). Always check the wheel alignment

GENERAL MAINTENANCE

after adjusting the secondary chain or altering the position of the rear wheel.

Wheel Alignment (Sidecar). Two plain boards about 5 ft. long are required. Each board must have one true edge. In addition, a third board of similar type, but about 4 ft. long, is needed.

Before checking the wheel alignment of a sidecar outfit, place the outfit on a smooth floor, preferably a concrete surface. Referring to Fig. 44, to

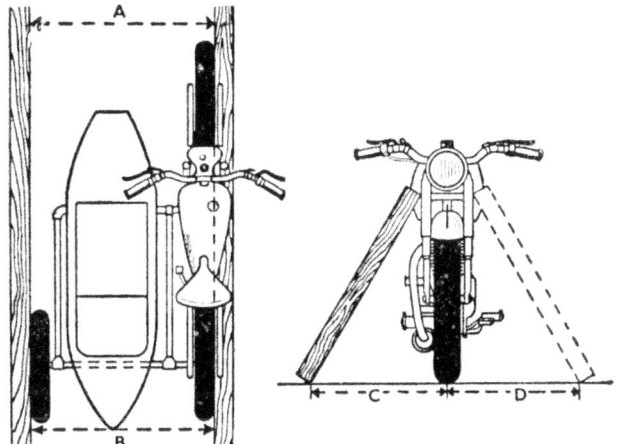

FIG. 44. CHECKING WHEEL ALIGNMENT ON A SIDECAR OUTFIT
If alignment is correct, dimension A is about $\frac{3}{4}$ in. less than dimension B and dimension C about 1 in. more than dimension D.

check that all three wheels of the A.J.S. are running in track, place one of the long boards alongside the front and rear tyres of the motor-cycle and verify that the board contacts the front and rear of each tyre, as when checking alignment on a solo machine. Move the handlebars until the best contact is obtained.

Without disturbing the board placed alongside the motor-cycle tyres place the second long board so that its true edge contacts the sidecar tyre, as illustrated in Fig. 44. Then, with a steel measuring-tape, check dimensions (A) and (B), with the tape as close to the tyres as practicable. To obtain the best results, dimension (A) should be about $\frac{3}{4}$ in. less than dimension (B). If the motor-cycle and sidecar wheels are dead parallel, there is a tendency for the sidecar outfit to pull towards the left. Some "toe-in" is necessary.

Having checked the three wheels for alignment, see whether the motor-cycle *leans slightly outwards*. Referring to Fig. 44, take the 4 ft. board and rest it at a given point against the upper part of the telescopic front forks.

Mark the floor where the edge of the board touches it. Then rest the board on the opposite side of the forks with its upper end in exactly the corresponding position and again mark the floor where the lower edge of the board touches. With the steel measuring-tape, check dimensions (C) and (D). If the machine is truly vertical, these two dimensions are quite equal. If the motor-cycle leans *outwards* the correct amount, dimension (C) should be about 1 in. more than dimension (D). To prevent drag on right-hand bends the sidecar axle should be about 1 in. in front of the rear-wheel spindle. Follow exactly the sidecar maker's advice when fitting a sidecar.

The sidecar chassis fittings on a new A.J.S. outfit sometimes take a permanent "set," causing the motor-cycle to lean slightly towards the sidecar. This must be rectified by adjusting the attachment arms.

Tyre Treads. It is a good plan occasionally to jack-up both wheels and carefully inspect the tyre treads for small stones or flints, which should be removed.

BRAKES

Good Braking Is Vital. Always keep both brakes in efficient working order. Your very life may depend on this. On all 1955–65 models it is possible to—

(1) Adjust the position of the rear-brake pedal to suit individual requirements.

(2) Make a hand adjustment of both brakes.

On 1955–63 models a thrust-pin adjustment for the brake shoes is also provided. Badly worn linings should always be renewed.

To Adjust Brake Pedal Position (1955). If the existing position of the rear-brake pedal on your A.J.S. does not suit you it is possible to vary the pedal position within narrow limits (*see* Fig. 45) by means of the adjuster bolt (4) screwed into the heel of the pedal and secured by the lock-nut (5).

If it is desired to raise somewhat the rear-brake pedal (1), *unscrew* the adjuster bolt (4) after first loosening the lock-nut (5). The best adjustment for normal purposes is to set the adjuster bolt so that, with the foot clear of the pedal, the arm of the brake pedal just clears the underside of the footrest arm.

Altering the position of the brake pedal necessarily moves the rear-brake rod (3) and therefore makes it necessary to check and if necessary alter the adjustment of the rear brake as described on page 96.

To Adjust Brake Pedal (1956–65). On the 1956–65 models the rear-brake pedal is located by a spring-loaded sprag which is positioned between the stop on the pedal and the leg of the spring which is of the hairpin type and fitted to the inner side of the pedal boss (*see* Fig. 46).

Fig. 45. ADJUSTMENT FOR REAR-BRAKE PEDAL (1955)
Note the detachable domed clutch-cover fitted to 1955–7 models.

KEY TO FIG. 45

1. Rear-brake pedal.
2. Grease nipple.
3. Rod to shoe expander-lever
4. Pedal adjuster bolt.
5. Lock-nut for item 4.

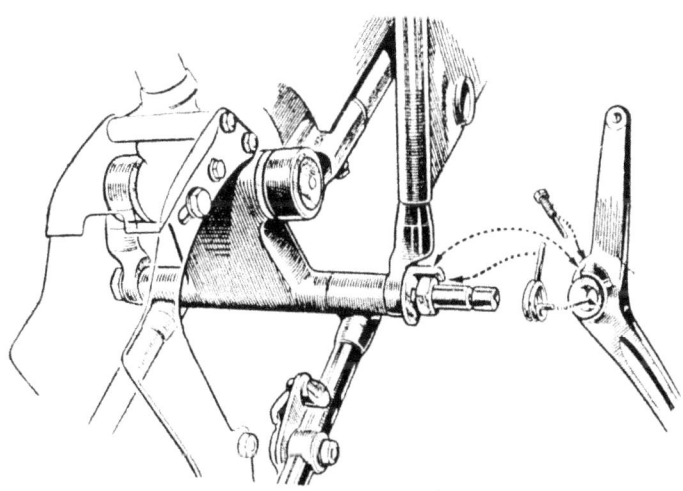

Fig. 46. ADJUSTMENT FOR REAR-BRAKE PEDAL (1956–65)

96   THE BOOK OF THE A.J.S.

To adjust the position of the brake pedal, first loosen the nut on the off-side of the pedal spindle. Then move the pedal to the best position (normally such that the pedal just clears the footrest rubber when the brake is off). Afterwards retighten securely the nut on the off-side of the spindle, and check the adjustment of the rear brake. After altering the brake pedal position re-set the stop-lamp switch which is adjustable.

Adjustment of Rear Brake. It is advisable to check the rear brake adjustment occasionally. Unless considerable wear of the brake-shoe

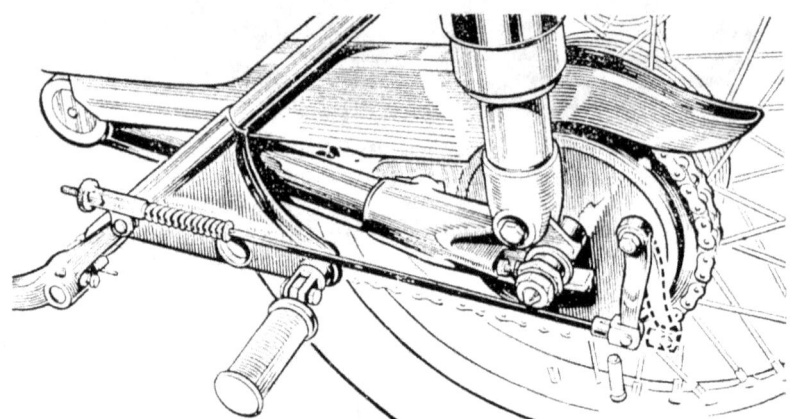

FIG. 47. REAR BRAKE ADJUSTMENT ON 1956–63 MODELS
Where the brake-rod adjustment is exhausted a brake-shoe adjustment (1955–63) is needed. On 1955, 1964–5 models the hand adjuster is at the rear.

linings has taken place, it is generally found that only a hand brake adjustment is called for. The adjustment is correct when the brake-shoe linings are almost in contact with the rear-brake drum when the pedal is in the "Off" position.

To make a rear brake adjustment, jack the A.J.S. up on its rear or centre stand. Then on 1955 models to eliminate "lost motion," screw the hand adjuster (2) at the rear of the brake rod (*see* Fig. 52) farther on to the rod until slight friction is felt between the brake linings and the brake drum when the rear wheel is spun with the gear-change lever in "neutral." Having obtained contact between the linings and drum, *unscrew* the self-locking adjuster nut *two complete turns.*

On 1956–65 "swinging-arm" models the rear brake adjustment is similar to that just described for the 1955 models, but on the 1956–63 models the hand-type adjuster is on the front end of the brake rod (*see* Fig. 47). It is advisable after tightening the adjuster so that the brake linings just contact the drum, to *unscrew* the self-locking adjuster nut *five complete turns.*

GENERAL MAINTENANCE 97

Where it is not possible to adjust the rear brake by means of the hand adjustment, owing to a poor angle between the brake-expander lever and rod, it is satisfactory (if the brake linings are serviceable) to make a brake shoe adjustment (*see* below).

Adjustment of Front Brake. This adjustment, like that of the rear brake, should be checked occasionally. It is satisfactory when the brake-shoe

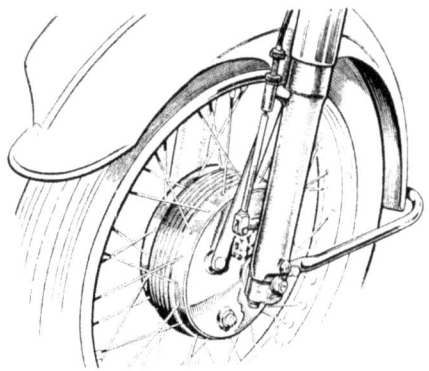

FIG. 48. FRONT BRAKE ADJUSTMENT ON 1955–63 MODELS

On 1964–5 models a similar type of adjustment is provided, but on the 350 c.c. model it is on the off-side of the machine lower down. Where the cable adjuster thread is exhausted as shown above it is desirable on 1955–63 models to make a brake shoe thrust-pin adjustment.

linings are nearly in contact with the front-brake drum when the handlebar lever is not operated. Unless considerable wear of the brake linings, or of the cable control (or of both) develops, a minor hand adjustment should be sufficient. This is effected in the following manner—

The adjustment for the front brake is usually provided on the near-side of the telescopic forks. First jack up the A.J.S. on both its stands (centre stand, 1956 onwards). Then slacken the knurled lock-nut. Now take up "lost motion" by unscrewing the knurled cable-adjuster nut until the brake-shoe linings just contact the brake drum when the front wheel is spun by hand. Finally, screw down the knurled adjuster *two complete turns* and tighten the lock-nut securely.

If hand adjustment of the front brake is no longer possible owing to the poor angle between the brake-expander lever and the cable, a brakeshoe adjustment should be made on 1955–63 models.

Brake Shoe Adjustment (1955–63 Models). After a very considerable mileage continuous adjustment of the hand adjuster for the front-brake cable or rear-brake rod causes the brake cam to become positioned so that the available leverage is considerably reduced, causing a serious loss in brake efficiency. To remedy this it is necessary to make a shoe adjustment. A hardened and detachable thrust pin is fitted to one end of each brake shoe and shims can be fitted beneath the thrust pin as and when required, thereby increasing the effective height of the pin and compensating for brake lining wear.

Referring to Fig. 49, it is necessary only to remove the thrust pin (1)

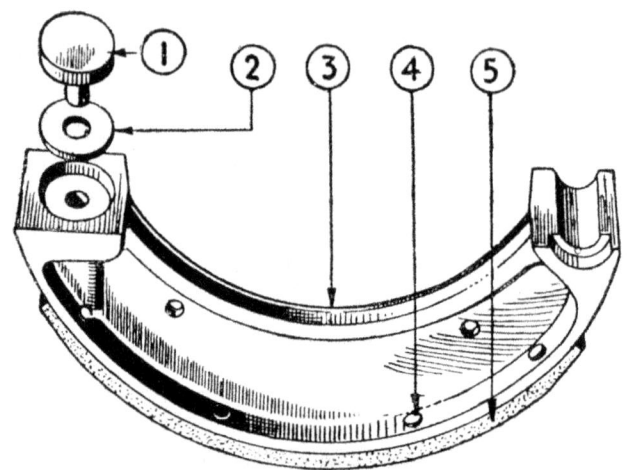

FIG. 49. SHOWING 1955–63 BRAKE SHOE WITH THRUST-PIN ADJUSTMENT

KEY TO FIG. 49

1. Hardened thrust-pin.
2. Shim washer.
3. Brake shoe.
4. Rivet (8 per set) for securing lining.
5. Brake-shoe lining.

from the brake shoe (3) and then fit a shim washer (2) beneath the hardened thrust-pin. Eight shim washers (Part No. 000174) are contained in the tool kit of each new A.J.S. to permit adjustment if and when necessary.

Having effected a brake shoe adjustment, slacken off the hand adjuster and make the required brake adjustment. See that the adjustment is not too close. The wheel must be able to turn without any friction.

Brake Shoe Interchangeability. Although it is permissible to fit the rear-brake shoes and springs to the front-brake cover plate, this is not desirable without good reason. The brake shoes on the *same* cover plate are *not* interchangeable.

Positioning of Front-Brake Cover Plate (1955–63). The front-brake cover plate is secured to the spindle with an internal and external nut.

If the front wheel has been removed (*see* page 117), it is important, before replacing it in the "Teledraulic" front forks, to position the internal nut correctly.

On 1955–63 models position the internal nut so that, when the cover plate is applied, the outer face of the plate is flush with the edge of the wheel-hub shell.

Fit the external nut so that its hexagonal side abuts the front-brake cover plate.

Centralizing Brake Shoes (1955–63). Where a front- or rear-brake cover plate has been removed and the shoe assembly dismantled or disturbed, it is advisable to centralize the two shoes in the brake drum during assembly. This ensures that equal pressure is exerted on the drum by *both* linings. Lack of centralizing is often accompanied by an irritating squeak occurring during brake application.

Centralize the brake shoes before replacing the front wheel, or, where the rear wheel is concerned, after replacing the rear wheel.

To effect centralizing, first loosen the nut securing the brake cover plate to the spindle of the wheel. Also (on 1955 and subsequent models) loosen slightly the nut on the fulcrum stud for the front wheel. Next increase the leverage of the shoe expander operating-lever by slipping a box spanner over the lever. Exert pressure on the spanner to expand the shoes to their full extent and simultaneously tighten the nut on the spindle so as to secure the brake cover plate to the spindle. Also tighten (1955 onwards) the nut on the fulcrum stud for the front wheel.

THE TRANSMISSION

The Four-speed Gearbox. Apart from attending to lubrication as described on page 49 in Chapter IV, the gearbox itself needs no attention for thousands of miles. After a very big mileage it may need stripping-down and thoroughly overhauling. The gearbox is best returned to the makers or an authorized repairer for this work.

All 1955–6 A.J.S. models have a four-speed Burman gearbox and multi-plate clutch. On 1957–65 models a new gearbox, designed and made by Associated Motor Cycles, Ltd., is fitted. This compact unit incorporates some well-proved Norton features, and the clutch centre embodies a transmission shock-absorber of the rubber-block and vane type. Fig. 50 shows the internal details.

Checking Tension of Primary Chain (1955–65). The tension of the primary chain should be checked occasionally and, then if necessary, adjusted. Adjustment of the primary chain must always be effected *before* that of the secondary chain, as it alters the tension of the secondary chain automatically.

To check the adjustment, place the machine on the centre stand and remove the inspection cap from the oil-bath chain case (*see* page 52). Then with the fingers check the chain whip (total up-and-down movement) mid-way between the two sprockets, with the chain in its tightest position. The whip should be approximately ⅜ in.

Adjusting Primary Chain (1955). If an adjustment is needed, slacken the nut on the right-hand side of the gearbox upper fixing-bolt. Also

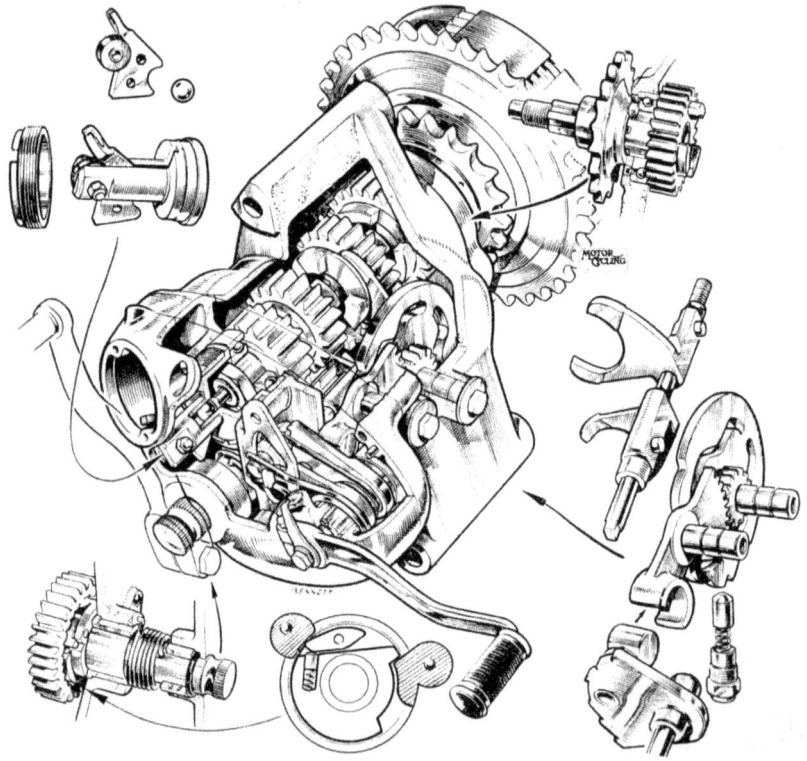

FIG. 50. SHOWING INTERNAL DETAILS OF THE 1957–65 A.M.C. FOUR-SPEED GEARBOX, ALSO THE FOOT GEAR CHANGE AND CLUTCH OPERATING MECHANISM
(*Courtesy of "Motor Cycling"*)

loosen a few (2–3) turns the front nut on the gearbox adjuster eye-bolt. Then screw up the rear nut on the adjuster eye-bolt until the chain is felt to be quite taut, as checked with the fingers inserted through the inspection-cap orifice. Now loosen the rear nut on the adjuster eye-bolt and carefully tighten the front nut until the chain tension is found to be correct. Tighten the rear nut to lock the assembly. Afterwards tighten the nut on the gearbox top fixing-bolt. Replace the inspection cap on the oil-bath chain case, and check the tension of the secondary chain.

Primary Chain Adjustment (1956–65). On all 1956–65 models a snap-on cover between the rear engine plates gives instant access to a redesigned adjustment. Referring to Fig. 51, if a primary chain adjustment is called

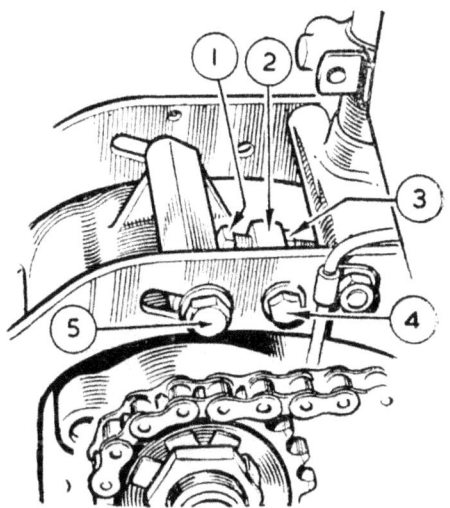

FIG. 51. PRIMARY CHAIN ADJUSTMENT ON 1956–65 MODELS
The snap-on cover has been removed to show the adjustment.

for, first loosen the nut on bolt (5) and slacken lock-nut (3). Now screw the adjuster bolt (1) *into* the crosshead (2) to take up primary-chain slackness. Then pull on the secondary chain to move the 4-speed gearbox and tighten the primary chain until it is correctly tensioned ($\frac{3}{8}$ in. whip), as checked with the fingers through the inspection-cap hole on the oil-bath chain case. If the chain is over-tightened, screw the adjuster bolt (1) *out of* the crosshead (2).

After correctly retensioning the primary chain, retighten lock-nut (3) and also the nut on bolt (5). Finally replace the inspection cap on the oil-bath chain case, replace the snap-on cover over the engine plates, and check the tension of the secondary chain.

To Adjust Secondary Chain (1955–65 Models). Occasionally check that the tension of the secondary chain is correct. With the machine on its centre stand there should be $1\frac{1}{8}$ in. total up-and-down movement at the centre of the lower chain-run, with the chain in its tightest position. This whip is reduced to about ½ in. when the rider is seated and the wheels are resting on the ground.

Where a fully enclosed chain case (an optional extra) is fitted remove the rubber grummet in the case to check chain tension. Note that where the secondary chain is fully enclosed the maintenance of correct chain tension is particularly important, otherwise the chain is likely to contact the chain case.

Before making an adjustment of the secondary chain, always check and if necessary adjust the tension of the primary chain (*see* pages 100, 101). After adjusting the secondary chain always check the rear brake adjustment (*see* page 96).

On 1955 and later models an adjuster screw and lock-nut (*see* Fig. 52)

FIG. 52. REAR BRAKE ADJUSTMENT (1955) AND SECONDARY CHAIN ADJUSTMENT (1955–65)

KEY TO FIG. 52

1. Grease nipple for brake expander bush.
2. Hand adjuster for rear brake (*see also* Fig. 47).
3. Spindle-end nut.
4. Lock-nut (brake cover plate).
5. Chain adjuster-screw.
6. Lock-nut for screw 5.

are provided on the front side of each rear fork-end. To make a secondary chain adjustment (with the machine on its centre stand), loosen the spindle-end nut (3) on the near side; slacken the adjacent lock-nut (4) for the brake drum dummy-spindle. Now loosen the lock-nut (6), on each side, and screw *out* the chain adjuster-screws (5) as required to tighten the chain correctly. Note that it is essential to unscrew both chain adjuster-screws *the same amount*, and before tightening the lock-nuts and spindle-end nut it is desirable to check the alignment of the wheels (*see* page 92).

GENERAL MAINTENANCE 103

Removing Secondary Chain (1955-65). On 1955 and later spring-frame models the guard for the secondary chain shrouds the chain very closely and the procedure outlined below is recommended if you wish to remove the chain without first removing the chain guard.

Position the motor-cycle on its centre stand and rotate the rear wheel until the connecting-link on the chain is close to the rear-wheel sprocket. Remove the link. Now pass a piece of string (about 10 ft. long) through the centre hole of the end link of the top run. Draw both ends of the string together and tie them together. Keeping the string taut at the rear end with one hand, with the other hand pull the bottom run of the chain backwards. When the end of the top run of the chain leaves the gearbox sprocket the string will be left attached, one strand lying on each side of the sprocket teeth. When the chain is finally clear, cut the string on one side at a position approximately 1 ft. from where it is looped through the chain link. Pending the replacement of the secondary chain, leave the string in position.

Replacing Secondary Chain (1955-65). Push the longer cut end of the above-mentioned string through the hole in the centre of the chain end-link and tie both the loose ends of the string together. Pull the string from the rear end, while guiding the chain up on to the gearbox sprocket teeth. Keep pulling until the chain encircles the rear-wheel sprocket. Afterwards remove the string and replace the chain connecting-link. Be careful when doing this to fit the spring link correctly (*see* Fig. 58).

The Dynamo Chain (1955-7). The tension of the chain which drives the dynamo (*see* Fig. 55) should be checked *monthly* and adjusted if necessary in accordance with the instructions given on page 29 of Chapter III. It is not necessary to remove the oil-bath chain case cover as shown in Fig. 55.

Harsh Transmission (1955-6). If harshness in the transmission develops, immediately check the level of oil in the oil-bath chain case. Provided the oil level is maintained correctly, proper lubrication of the faces of the two cams of the shock absorber (*see* Fig. 55) fitted to the engine shaft is ensured. Top up the oil level, using engine oil, as required (*see* page 43). If harshness continues, remove the outer half of the oil-bath chain case and dismantle and lubricate the components of the shock-absorber.

The Engine Shaft Shock-absorber (1955-6). When assembling the engine shaft shock-absorber, fit the components in this order: (*a*) the spacing collar, which is a sliding fit on the driving-side flywheel mainshaft and lies between the bearing of this shaft and the engine sprocket; (*b*) the engine sprocket, which is integral with the dynamo driving-sprocket; (*c*) the shock-absorber cam which overrides the engine sprocket cam under the influence of the engine impulses; (*d*) the shock-absorber spring; (*e*) the cap washer, which retains the shock-absorber spring; (*f*) the sleeve lock-nut, which must be firmly tightened against the driving-side flywheel mainshaft.

The Clutch Shock-absorber (1957–65 Models). The 1957–65 engines do not incorporate an engine shaft shock-absorber, but instead a transmission shock-absorber embodied in the clutch centre. As may be seen in Fig. 53, the clutch shock-absorber has six rubber blocks. After a

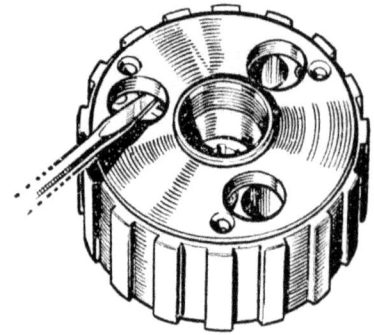

FIG. 53. SHOWING (LEFT) VIEW INSIDE THE CLUTCH SHOCK-ABSORBER COMPARTMENT AFTER REMOVING THREE SCREWS AND PRISING OFF THE STEEL COVER PLATE AS SHOWN (RIGHT)

very considerable mileage it may become necessary to remove and renew these blocks.

To remove the six rubber blocks, first remove the domed clutch cover (1957 models) from the oil-bath chain case or the oil-bath chain case cover (1958–65 models). Also remove the clutch spring pressure-plate (*see* Fig. 54), the springs, and the spring cups. Next remove the three securing-screws and prise off the steel cover-plate from the clutch shock-absorber compartment. Then remove the rubber blocks.

To compress the thick rubbers while extracting the thinner ones, a useful tool is a "C"-shaped spanner (engaging two slots in the clutch centre), having an extension handle fitted to it. To use this tool, engage fourth gear, apply the rear brake, position the tool, and pull the handle upwards (opposite to the direction of clutch rotation). Then with a short piece of hub spoke (pointed at the end), prise out the thin rubber blocks, followed by the thicker ones. Fit new rubber blocks in the reverse order of removal. Note that, if the clutch centre is removed, it is necessary to use a tool such as a gearbox main-shaft to hold the clutch centre while extracting the rubber blocks.

Clutch Slip. This must be avoided at all costs, as it causes damage and overheating, and spoils performance. Sometimes it is due to incorrect adjustment of the clutch springs (see page 107), but generally it is due to insufficient free movement in the clutch operating-mechanism, which can be felt at the handlebar clutch-lever. A method of testing for clutch slip is to place the machine on its stand, start up the engine, engage top gear, and then apply the rear brake. It should be possible to pull up the engine, even on full throttle, without the occurrence of clutch slip.

1955–6 Burman Clutch Adjustment. With the clutch correctly adjusted there should be $\frac{1}{8}$ in.–$\frac{3}{16}$ in. free movement of the clutch operating-cable. To check this free movement, lift the outer casing of the cable at the point where it enters the adjuster screw on the kick-starter casing cover, and see if you can move the casing freely with the fingers up and down the above amount. Also check the backlash at the handlebar lever.

Should there be excessive free movement of the clutch control-cable (resulting in clutch drag and noisy gear-changing), adjust the clutch control in the following manner. First slacken the lock-nut on the clutch cable adjuster-screw (1, Fig. 26) and screw in the adjuster screw (by turning its hexagon) as far as possible to ensure that the internal operating-lever is in its normal position. Next remove the dome-shaped clutch cover which is secured by eight screws. Now with the plug spanner, slacken the large central lock-nut, and with a screwdriver gently screw in the thrust cup to which the lock-nut is fitted, until contact with the thrust rod (inside the gearbox mainshaft) can be felt. Then unscrew the thrust cup *exactly one-half turn*. Afterwards firmly retighten the central lock-nut. When doing this be careful not to allow the thrust cup to turn. Replace the dome-shaped clutch cover and effect the final clutch adjustment by unscrewing the external cable adjuster-screw until the correct amount of free movement of the clutch cable-casing (see above) is obtained. Finally secure the adjuster screw by tightening the lock-nut.

If insufficient free movement of the clutch cable (caused by wear of the friction inserts) is present, clutch-slip results and an immediate adjustment must be made. Slacken off the external cable-adjuster, remove the domed-clutch-cover, loosen the large central lock-nut, and then unscrew the thrust cup (to which the nut is fitted) a turn or two. Afterwards screw in the thrust cup until, as previously mentioned, the cup makes contact with the thrust rod inside the gearbox mainshaft. Then unscrew the thrust cup *exactly one-half turn*, and retighten the lock-nut. Finally replace the domed clutch cover and make a control-cable adjustment by means of the external adjuster screw and lock-nut until the required free movement of $\frac{1}{8}$ in.–$\frac{3}{16}$ in. is obtained.

1957–65 A.M.C. Clutch Adjustment. All 1957–65 A.J.S. models have a four-speed gearbox and multi-plate clutch made by Associated Motor Cycles, Ltd. Details of the multi-plate clutch and the clutch operating-mechanism are shown in Fig. 54. To avoid clutch-slip or drag (caused by insufficient or excessive free movement of the cable), it is essential to maintain $\frac{1}{8}$ in.–$\frac{3}{16}$ in. free movement of the clutch operating-cable.

Note that *insufficient* free movement will quickly ruin the clutch inserts and can generate sufficient heat to soften the clutch springs. Should clutch slip occur, make an *immediate* check on the free movement. *Excessive* free movement of the cable, besides causing clutch drag, also causes noisy gear-changing. Both are objectionable.

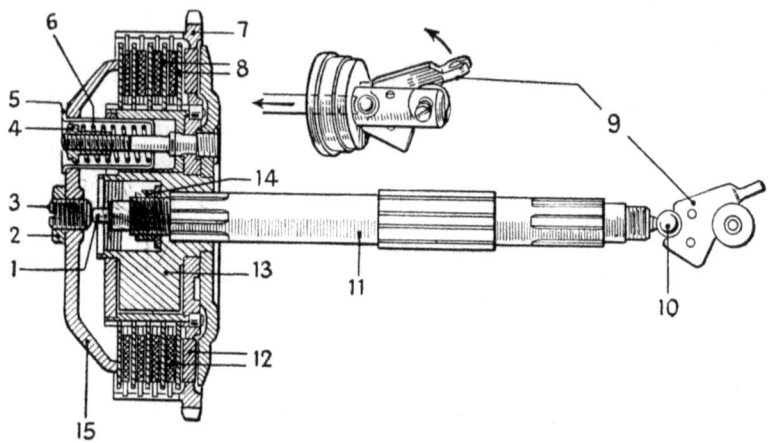

FIG. 54. DETAILS OF A.M.C. MULTI-PLATE CLUTCH AND OPERATING MECHANISM (1957–65 MODELS)

KEY TO FIG. 54

1. Long thrust-rod.
2. Lock-nut for 3.
3. Thrust cup.
4. Spring adjustment-nut.
5. Clutch-spring cup.
6. Clutch spring (three).
7. Clutch sprocket.
8. Steel plain-plates.
9. Clutch operating-lever.
10. Steel ball.
11. Gearbox mainshaft.
12. Friction-insert plates.
13. Clutch centre.
14. Nut securing 13.
15. Spring pressure-plate.

To check for the correct free movement of the clutch operating-cable, lift the outer casing where it enters the adjustable cable-stop on the cover of the kick-starter casing. Total up-and-down movement should be as stated in a previous paragraph.

To rectify *insufficient* free movement of the operating cable (caused by wear of the friction inserts causing the plates to close up), first loosen the lock-nut and slacken off the adjustable cable-stop on the cover of the kick-starter casing. Next remove (1957 models) the domed cover (secured by eight screws) from the oil-bath chain case (Fig. 45). On 1958 and later models remove the screwed cap from the oil-bath chain case cover. Referring to Fig. 54, with the sparking-plug spanner provided in the tool kit, loosen the lock-nut (2). Then with a screwdriver *unscrew* the thrust cup (3) a turn or two, and afterwards carefully screw it in until you feel it contacts the end of the long thrust-rod (1). Having done this, *unscrew* the thrust cup (3) *exactly one-half turn*, retighten the lock-nut (2),* and screw home firmly the domed clutch cover (1955-7) or the screwed cap (1958-65). Finally adjust the cable-stop until the required free movement ($\frac{1}{8}$ in.–$\frac{3}{16}$ in.) of the operating cable is obtained, and retighten the cable-stop lock-nut. Check for backlash at the clutch lever on the handlebars.

To rectify *excessive* free movement of the clutch operating-cable, loosen the lock-nut on the adjustable cable-stop and, referring to Fig. 54, screw in the stop as far as possible to ensure that the operating lever (9) is in its normal position. Next slacken the lock-nut (2). With a screwdriver gently *screw in* the thrust cup (3) until you feel that it contacts the end of the long thrust rod (1). Then *unscrew* the thrust cup *exactly one-half turn* and finally retighten the lock-nut (2).* Refit the domed clutch-cover on the oil-bath chain case, and make the final adjustment by means of the adjustable cable-stop. When these operations have been carried out, and the clutch adjustment is found to be correct, the cable-stop lock-nut should then be retightened.

To Adjust Clutch Springs (1955-6 Models). A spring adjustment may be necessary if clutch slip persists in spite of the free movement of the clutch cable being correct. Remove the domed cover (secured by eight screws) from the oil-bath chain case (*see* Fig. 45). This gives access to the clutch-spring adjuster nuts, shown at *P* in Fig. 57.

To make an adjustment on 1955-6 models, use the slotted screwdriver provided on one of the spanners in the tool kit. *Screw in fully each adjuster nut and then unscrew it exactly four turns.* Then check (*see* page 104) whether clutch slip still exists. Further tightening is undesirable, especially as this causes the clutch to be rather heavy to operate. Should tightening beyond the recommended amount be necessary in order to cure clutch slip, this indicates that: (*a*) the springs have lost their proper tension; or (*b*) the clutch inserts are worn so badly that they need renewal; or (*c*) the inserts have become impregnated with oil.

Should oil on the clutch plates be the cause of slip, soak the plates in petrol and afterwards allow to dry. Roughen glazed inserts with some sand-paper. After adjusting the clutch springs, or checking the adjustment, replace the domed cover.

To Adjust Clutch Springs (1957-65). As on 1955-6 models, an adjustment may be required if clutch slip continues in spite of the adjustment

---

* When retightening the lock-nut (2, Fig. 54) be careful to see that the adjustable thrust cup does not also rotate.

of the control cable being correct (*see* page 106). To obtain access to the clutch-spring adjuster nuts, on 1957 models, remove the domed cover (secured by eight screws) from the oil-bath chain case. On 1958–65 models remove the outer half of the oil-bath chain case. Care must be taken when doing this.

Referring to Fig. 54, remove the spring adjusting nuts (4), withdraw the three springs (6), and the spring cups (5). Then check that the spring cups do *not* contact the holes machined in the steel plate for the clutch shock-absorber assembly (*see* Fig. 53). Contact is indicated by burrs formed on the cups. Remove any burrs with a fine file and apply a little graphite grease on the cups before replacing them.

Check the free length of the clutch springs which should be $1\frac{7}{8}$ in. If the free length is found to be $\frac{3}{16}$ in.–$\frac{1}{4}$ in. below the correct length, replace the clutch springs. After replacing the spring cups and springs, *screw in the adjuster nuts until their heads are flush with the spring cups*. Finally replace the domed cover (1957) or the outer half of the oil-bath chain case (1958–65).

Removing Outer Half of Oil-bath Chain Case (1955–7). Place a suitable receptacle beneath the oil-bath to receive the oil as it runs out. Remove the near-side footrest arm. The next step is to remove the screw which binds the metal band at the rear of the oil-bath chain case, and detach the band. Take off the rubber oil-sealing band, and remove the nut and plain washer from the bolt projecting from the centre of the chain case. Finally withdraw the outer half of the chain case. This exposes the primary chain, clutch, dynamo chain, and engine shaft shock-absorber (*see* Fig. 55).

Removing Outer Half of Oil-bath Chain Case (1958–65). A very strong polished aluminium oil-bath chain case is fitted to the coil-ignition models. As may be seen in Fig. 56, the rotor of the Lucas RM15 alternator is secured to the engine shaft and the stator is bolted to the outer half of the chain case. Attached to the stator is an important cable which passes through the inner half of the chain case. Care must be taken not to damage this cable.

Remove the snap-on cover between the rear engine plates and disconnect the three snap connectors. Also remove the near-side footrest. Unscrew the knurled adjuster nut from the rod operating the rear brake. To catch engine oil which will drain from the chain case when the outer half is removed, lay a suitable drip tray beneath the chain case. Now remove the drain plug and allow all the oil (12 ounces) in the chain case to drain off. Also unscrew the oil-bath inspection cap (*see* page 52), and remove the nut located in the centre of the outer half of the chain case. Then remove the 14 screws which secure the outer half of the chain case.

With the rear brake pedal depressed, withdraw the outer half of the chain case *squarely* so as to prevent damaging the stator windings. Also

GENERAL MAINTENANCE

be most careful not to impose any strain on the stator cable. Thread each connector through the rubber grummet in the oil-bath chain case, one at a time.

Replacing Outer Half of Oil-bath Chain Case (1955-7). Check that the faces of both halves of the chain case are clean and that the rubber and metal bands are both clean and undamaged. The rubber band is of the endless type and of larger section than the earlier version. Position the outer half of the chain case so that its exterior edge coincides exactly with

FIG. 55. OIL-BATH CHAIN CASE WITH OUTER HALF REMOVED (1955-7)
This view shows: he engine shaft shock-absorber, the primary chain, the clutch, and the dynamo driving chain. The engine shaft shock-absorber and the dynamo chain are omitted on 1958-64 models (see Fig. 56).

that of the back half, and then fit the endless rubber band. Next fit the metal band. Begin at the front of the chain case and draw together the two free ends of the band with one hand, while inserting the binding screw with the other hand. When tightening the binding screw, apply light blows (with a rubber mallet) all round the exterior of the band. This will cause the metal band to creep on the rubber band and enable the binding screw to be fully tightened down. Replace the nut and washer on the centre fixing bolt, replace the footrest arm and finally remove the inspection cap from the oil-bath chain case, pour in engine oil (page 43) to the correct level (page 51), and replace the inspection cap.

Leakage from Oil-bath (1955-7). If leakage be detected after replacing and replenishing the oil-bath chain case, this may be due to one or both faces of the case being damaged or distorted. Both faces should fit closely to a surface plate and, if there is any suspicion of distortion due to accidental impact prior to assembly, a check with a surface plate should be made. Another possible cause of oil leakage is imperfect registering of the two joint faces during assembly. Great care must be taken to ensure *exact* registering of the halves, without which an oil-tight oil-bath is unobtainable. It is also essential to see that the rubber band is correctly positioned, and that the contacting faces are scrupulously clean.

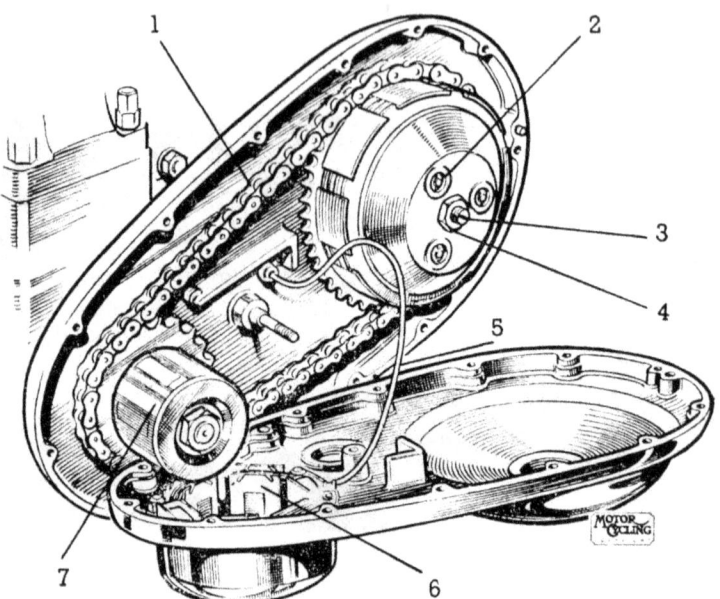

Fig. 56. Oil-bath Chain Case With Outer Half Removed (1958–65)
No engine shaft shock-absorber is included, the transmission shock-absorber being included in the clutch.

1. Primary chain.
2. Spring adjustment nuts.
3. Adjustable thrust cup.
4. Lock-nut for 3.
5. Stator lead.
6. Stator.
7. Rotor.

(*By courtesy of "Motor Cycling"*)

Replacing Outer Half of Oil-bath Chain Case (1958 Onwards). First check that the paper washer is undamaged. Offer up the outer half of the chain case and gently take up the slack of the stator lead (*see* Fig. 56) by pulling gently on the lead from the back of the inner half of the chain case. Locate the outer half of the case with the central nut and tighten the nut lightly.

Replace the 14 securing screws and tighten them first in a diagonal order, and then all round the case. Now tighten firmly the central fixing nut, and replenish the oil-bath chain case with suitable engine oil to the

GENERAL MAINTENANCE

correct level (*see* page 51). Finally replace the screwed inspection cap (*see* page 52), fit the rear-brake adjuster nut, and the near-side footrest, connect up the three snap connectors, and replace the snap-on cover between the rear engine plates.

To Remove a Clutch Control Cable. The following is the procedure for removing a clutch control cable where renewal is required. It applies to all 350 and 500 c.c. models. First remove the oil filler cap from the cover of the kick-starter case. Next screw home fully the clutch cable adjuster on top of the kick-starter case cover. Now disconnect the clutch cable inner wire from the clutch operating lever. This can be done through the oil filler cap orifice. Also disconnect the clutch inner wire from the clutch operating lever on the left-hand side of the handlebars. Then pull the cable lower end until it is clear of the motor-cycle. When doing this ease the cable through the frame cable clips.

To Replace Clutch Cable. Proceed in the reverse order of removal, and finally check and, if necessary, adjust the clutch operation as described on pages 105–7.

To Remove Primary Chain and Clutch Assembly (1955–6). The outer half of the oil-bath chain case must first be removed, as described on page 108. Referring to Fig. 57, remove by unscrewing uniformly (with end of spanner Part No. 017254) the four spring adjustment-nuts (P) and withdraw the clutch spring pressure-plate (F), complete with the four springs (M) and spring cups (R). Now remove the spring link from the primary chain and take the chain off the sprockets.

With top gear still engaged, again apply the rear brake and, after flattening the turned-up part of the locking-plate W located beneath the large central nut, unscrew the nut V retaining the clutch centre E to the sleeve on the gearbox mainshaft T. Remove the locking plate W and the plain washer X situated on the mainshaft behind the retaining nut. The entire clutch assembly may now be removed.

Withdraw the clutch assembly bodily by pulling it away from the gearbox mainshaft. The use of an extractor is generally quite unnecessary, as the clutch centre is a sliding fit on the mainshaft, but avoid losing any of the twenty-four clutch-bearing rollers which become free to move end-wise when the clutch centre and sprocket assembly (including the roller bearing retaining-washers) is withdrawn from the mainshaft.

To Remove Primary Chain and Clutch Assembly (1957–65). First remove the outer half of the oil-bath chain case (*see* page 108). Referring to Fig. 54, remove by unscrewing uniformly (with the end of spanner Part No. 017254) the spring adjustment-nuts (4), and take away the spring pressure-plate (15), complete with the three clutch springs (6) and the clutch-spring cups (5). Engage fourth gear and apply the rear brake. Then with a suitable box-spanner unscrew the nut (14) which secures the clutch centre (13) to the gearbox mainshaft (11). Disconnect the primary chain by removing the spring link, and remove the chain. Now pull

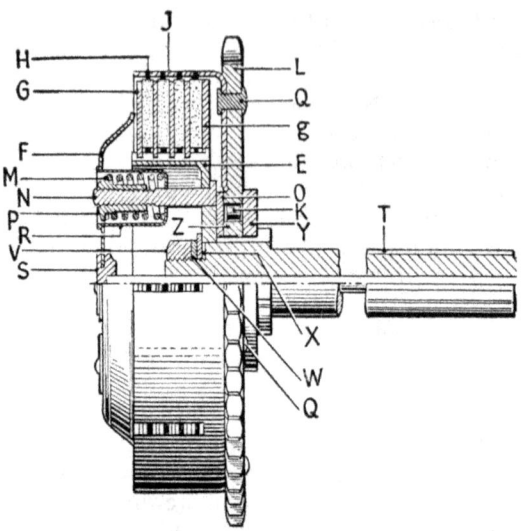

FIG. 57. DETAILS OF 1955-6 BURMAN MULTI-PLATE CLUTCH

KEY TO FIG. 57

E. Clutch centre.
F. Spring pressure-plate.
G,g. Steel plain-plates.
H. Friction plates (five, 500 c.c.).
J. Clutch case.
K. Roller-bearing rollers (24).
L. Clutch sprocket.
M. Clutch spring (four or five).
N. Stud for spring-adjustment nut.
O. Washer (thin) retaining roller-bearing.

P. Spring-adjustment nut.
Q. Rivet.
R. Spring cup (one of four).
S. Pressure-plate boss.
T. Gearbox mainshaft.
V. Nut retaining clutch-centre.
W. Locking plate.
X. Plain washer.
Y. Washer (thick) retaining roller-bearing.
Z. Roller-bearing ring.

away the complete clutch assembly from the mainshaft. An extractor is available if required.

Replacing Clutch Centre, Clutch Sprocket, and Primary Chain (1955-6). Referring to Fig. 57, fit the roller-bearing retaining-washer (Y) on the gearbox mainshaft spindle-sleeve. This is the thicker of the two retaining washers. Next replace the roller-bearing ring (Z) on the splined sleeve of the mainshaft and with thick grease position the twenty-four rollers (K) on the bearing ring. Replace the clutch sprocket (L) over the rollers.

Next fit to the gearbox mainshaft splined-sleeve the washer (O) retaining the roller bearing. This is the thinner of the two retaining washers. Then fit the clutch centre (*E*) to the splined sleeve of the mainshaft and push home. Afterwards replace in this order: the plain washer (*X*), the locking plate (*W*), and the nut (*V*) retaining the clutch centre. This nut cannot be fully tightened until the primary chain is fitted.

Replace the primary chain on the two sprockets, being careful that the spring link is correctly fitted (*see* Fig. 58). Now tighten very firmly the

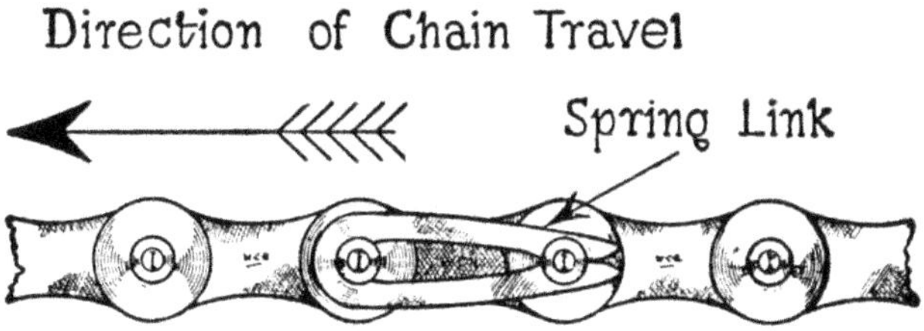

Direction of Chain Travel

Spring Link

FIG. 58. BE CAREFUL TO REPLACE A CHAIN SPRING-LINK CORRECTLY
The closed end must always face the direction of chain movement.

nut (*V*) which retains the clutch centre (*E*) to the mainshaft splined-sleeve. When tightening this nut, engage fourth gear and apply the rear brake to prevent the mainshaft turning. Turn up the edge of the locking plate (*W*) against a flat on the nut (*V*) retaining the clutch centre (*E*).

Fitting Clutch Plates and Springs (1955-6). Referring to Fig. 57, slide into position in the clutch case (*J*) attached to the clutch sprocket (*L*) a steel plain-plate (*g*). Make certain that the recessed part of this steel plate faces *towards* the clutch centre (*E*) and overhangs its flange (350 c.c. models).

Next slide into position one of the clutch friction-insert plates (*H*). Then fit a steel plain-plate, followed by another friction-insert plate, and so on, alternately, until the complete set of plates has been fitted. It should be noted that Models 16M, 16MS have five steel plain-plates and four friction-insert plates, whereas on Models 18, 18S the number is six and five respectively.

Now insert the four spring cups (*R*) into the spring pressure-plate (*F*) and offer up the pressure plate to the assembly. Fit the clutch springs (*M*) and retain the springs in place by screwing the four adjustment nuts (*P*) on to the studs (*N*). Tighten each nut a few turns as fitted, and then fully tighten in a uniform manner all four nuts. Afterwards slacken back each adjustment nut *four complete turns*. This is the standard spring-adjustment.

Finally check the adjustment of the primary chain and replace the outer half of the oil-bath chain case (*see* pages 100 and 109). Also verify that there is sufficient free movement in the clutch control (*see* page 105).

THE BOOK OF THE A.J.S.

Replacing Clutch Centre, Clutch Assembly, and Primary Chain (1957–65). Referring to Fig. 54, apply a little anti-centrifuge grease to the clutch-sprocket bearing, and position the complete clutch assembly* over the bearing rollers. Then fit the spring washer and the nut (14) securing the clutch centre (13) to the gearbox mainshaft (11). Tighten this nut lightly. Replace the primary chain, being careful to see that its spring link is correctly fitted (*see* Fig. 58). Engage fourth gear, apply the rear brake, and then tighten firmly the nut (14) securing the clutch centre (13), to the mainshaft. Position the spring pressure-plate (15) and fit in this order: the clutch-spring cups (5), the three clutch springs (6), and the spring adjustment-nuts (4). With the end of the appropriate spanner (Part No. 017254), screw home the adjustment-nuts until they are *just flush with the spring cups*. Finally check the primary chain adjustment (*see* page 99), and the clutch control adjustment (*see* page 105). Replace the outer half of the oil-bath chain case (*see* pages 109, 110).

To Remove Clutch Bearing (1957 Onwards). The clutch centre is secured to the clutch back plate by the three clutch studs and lock-nuts. The bearing can be removed after separating the clutch centre from the back plate. Before assembling, apply a little anti-centrifuge oil.

To Remove A.C. Rotor and Engine Sprocket (1958–65). First remove the outer half of the oil-bath chain case (*see* page 108). With fourth gear engaged, connect the rear-brake rod to the brake pedal. Next exert pressure on the rear-brake pedal and unscrew the lock-nut and nut which secure the rotor to the engine shaft. Then remove the washer and pull off the rotor shown at (7) in Fig. 56. The rotor is keyed to the engine shaft. Remove the front chain by withdrawing the connecting link. Remove the key for the rotor and also the distance piece ($1\frac{3}{32}$ in. wide). The engine sprocket can now be removed. It is not necessary to remove the distance piece behind it.

STEERING HEAD AND SUSPENSION

Handlebar Adjustment. The handlebars on all 1955–65 A.J.S. models are adjustable for angle to suit individual requirements. Loosen the three securing screws, and then adjust handlebars as required. After making the adjustment, be sure to retighten firmly the three securing screws.

The Steering Head Bearings (1955–65). On a new machine some initial bedding occurs during the first 100 miles' running, and the adjustment of the steering head should be checked when this mileage has been completed.

* Note that if the clutch assembly has been removed from the clutch centre, fit first the clutch sprocket, and then alternately steel plain-plates and friction-insert plates.

Subsequently it is only necessary to check the steering-head adjustment about every 3,000 miles.

The ball-bearing races of the steering head have spherical seats and are of the self-aligning type. Thus they are not designed to fit tightly in the steering-head lug.

Checking Steering-Head Adjustment. Jack up the front of the machine by placing a box beneath the crankcase to take all the weight off the front wheel. Then exert hand pressure upwards from the extreme ends of the handlebars. There should be no appreciable shake present and the steering head must be quite free to turn. If some shake is detected, adjust the steering head forthwith as described below.

To Adjust the Steering Head (1955–63). The following is the correct procedure for adjusting the steering head. It is assumed that the front wheel is not resting on the ground. Loosen the two pinch-screws located in the fork crown. Next slacken the domed lock-nut at the top of the steering column. Having slackened the lock-nut, screw down very gradually the lower adjusting nut for the steering head. This adjusting nut is located immediately below the lock-nut. While tightening the lower adjusting nut with the adjustable spanner, test for steering-head slackness by placing the fingers over the gap between the frame top-lug and the handlebar lug, while simultaneously exerting upward pressure on the front edge of the front mudguard.

Tighten the adjusting nut until the steering head is free to turn without perceptible up-and-down play. Afterwards tighten the domed lock-nut and the two pinch-screws in the fork crown. Finally withdraw the box or other packing from beneath the crankcase.

To Adjust Steering Head (1964–5). On 350 and 500 c.c. models having "Roadholder" front forks the following are the correct instructions for adjusting the steering head. With the front wheel clear of the ground, referring to Fig. 59, first loosen the two nuts (10) on the pinch studs (11) for the fork crown lug. Also loosen slightly the fork crown and column lock-nut (6). Then with a thin open-ended spanner, $1\frac{3}{8}$ in. across the flats, adjust the steering head adjuster nut (8) as required. The bearings should have no play but free movement. When making an adjustment, check for bearing play by trying to raise or lower the front wheel with one hand while using the fingers of the other hand around the handlebar lug where it meets the frame. If play exists some movement can be felt. After eliminating all play, retighten the securing nuts (6) and (10). Note: when checking the steering-head adjustment also check the fork filler plugs (7) for tightness.

The "Teledraulic" Front Forks (1955–63). Apart from checking the hydraulic fluid content every 5,000 miles (pages 55–6) and topping up if necessary, no attention is called for. No adjustment is necessary and all working parts are automatically lubricated by means of the hydraulic damping fluid. Unless damage has been accidentally sustained, the "Teledraulic" front forks should normally not require to be dismantled.

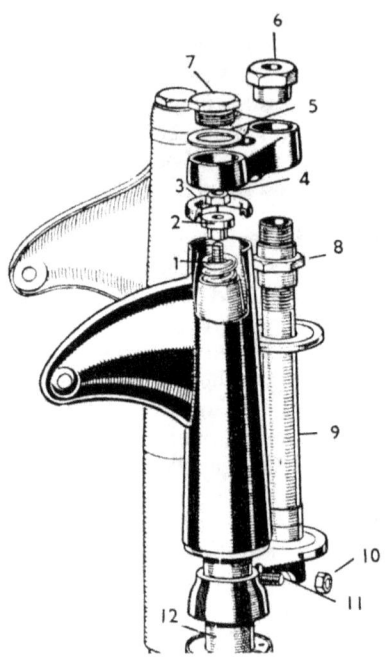

FIG. 59. SHOWING DETAILS OF UPPER PART OF "ROADHOLDER" FRONT FORKS AND THE STEERING HEAD ADJUSTMENT (1964–5)

KEY TO FIG. 59

1. Main spring.
2. Main spring locating bush.
3. Main tube top cover ring.
4. Nut for top of damper rod.
5. Washer for filler plug 7.
6. Fork crown and column lock-nut.
7. Filler plug.
8. Steering head adjuster nut.
9. Crown lug with column.
10. Nut for stud 11.
11. Pinch stud for crown lug.
12. Fork main tube.

However, after a very big mileage (say 30,000 miles) the oil seals and washers may require attention.

Having regard to the negligible attention normally required in respect of the "Teledraulic" front forks, the author has not included in this handbook detailed instructions for their stripping down and subsequent assembly. Those who on rare occasions require such information should refer to the appropriate instructions given in the instruction book issued with each new A.J.S. machine, or else contact the manufacturers.

GENERAL MAINTENANCE

The "Roadholder" Front Forks (1964-5). Apart from draining and replenishing the fork legs with damping oil at long intervals (*see* page 56), no maintenance is necessary. All internal parts are automatically lubricated and unless the front forks are damaged in an accident they are unlikely to require to be dismantled. For this reason instructions on stripping down the forks and reassembling them have not been included in this handbook.

"Swinging-Arm" Rear Suspension. As regards lubrication (*see* page 57), no attention should normally be required, except perhaps very occasionally on 1955-6 models with A.J.S. "Teledraulic" rear-suspension units, and then only if the telescopic legs become excessively lively.

On 1957-65 models (with Girling rear-suspension units) in the event of the legs becoming noisy in action, grease the outside of each spring as described on page 57. The springs on the Girling units are adjustable for loading. If you are above average weight, carry a pillion passenger, or regularly negotiate rough terrain, raise the base of each spring as required by turning with a "C" spanner *clockwise* the cam ring provided at the base of each telescopic lower member. Three positions (*see* Fig. 60) are obtainable, and the highest gives the maximum stiffness of springing. The application of a little thin oil to the cam ring facili-

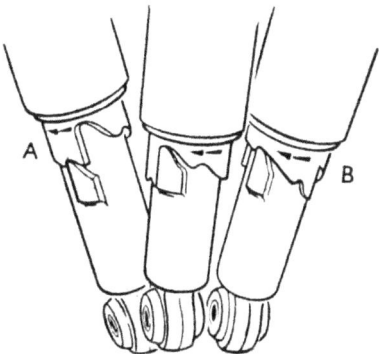

FIG. 60. SHOWING THE THREE SETTINGS FOR CAM RING ADJUSTMENT ON THE 1957-65 GIRLING REAR SUSPENSION UNITS

Positioning the cam ring as shown at A gives maximum stiffness of springing, and as shown at B the minimum stiffness of springing.

tates an adjustment. Should you fit a sidecar to your machine, it is advisable to change the suspension-unit springs, as stronger springs are generally desirable.

FRONT AND REAR WHEELS

Removing Front Wheel (1955-63 Models). Jack the machine up on its centre stand. Disconnect the yoke end of the front-brake cable from the brake-expander lever by removing the split-pin and retaining pin. On 1955-63 models remove the bolt securing the brake anchor-stay to the brake cover plate. Next loosen the nut on the left-hand side of the front-wheel spindle.

Remove the four nuts which clamp the fork-slider caps to the "Teledraulic" fork sliders. Detach both caps and place them aside separately, so that they may later be replaced exactly as before removal. These caps must *not* be interchanged. Apply pressure to the front wheel so as to reduce the effective height of the wheel spindle, and withdraw the wheel towards the front.

To Replace Front Wheel (1955-63 Models). Hold the left-hand fork-slider cap under the location on the front-wheel spindle, and offer up the front wheel assembly and cap so as to engage the cap with its two retaining studs. When replacing the front wheel remember to flatten the tyre so as to get the wheel spindle between the forward studs securing the slider caps. Fit the two nuts securing the left-hand fork-slider cap (and wheel spindle) and tighten the nuts lightly. Then fit the right-hand fork-slider cap and tighten lightly the cap securing-nuts. Make sure that the caps have not been interchanged and are fitted exactly as before. Now attach the brake anchor arm, firmly tighten the securing bolt, and replace the yoke end and pin.

Tighten lightly the nut on the left-hand side of the front-wheel spindle. Then firmly and evenly tighten the two nuts which secure the near-side fork-slider cap (and wheel spindle). Verify that the gaps, fore and aft, between the cap and the end of the fork slider are *exactly* equal. Ensuring that these gaps are equal is most important. Now firmly tighten the nut on the left-hand side of the front-wheel spindle, also the nuts securing the offside slider cap.

After Fitting Front Wheel (1955-63). If any stiffness in the action of the telescopic front forks is noticed after replacing the front wheel, slacken the nuts securing the off-side slider cap, operate the forks sharply up and down, and retighten the slider cap securing-nuts. This should cure the stiffness.

To Remove Front Wheel (1964-5 Models). First place the machine on its centre stand and remove the split pin and pin retaining the yoke end of the front-brake cable to the brake-expander lever. Unscrew the off-side wheel spindle nut (R.H. thread) and loosen the pinch stud nut on the near-side fork slider end.

Take the weight of the wheel in the left hand and withdraw the spindle from the near side by means of a tommy-bar placed through the hole in the head of the spindle. As the wheel is withdrawn take great care not to allow the brake plate to fall. If allowed to do so, the bevelled edge can be seriously damaged. Place the wheel spindle, brake plate, and dust cover in a clean receptacle to prevent contamination by grit.

To Replace Front Wheel (1964-5 Models). Reassemble in the reverse order of dismantling. Fit the brake plate to the brake drum and as the wheel is lifted into the "Roadholder" front forks, position the dust cover on the near-side and make sure that the torque stop on the brake plate engages the slot in the off-side fork leg. Remove all traces of rust from the wheel spindle and grease the spindle. With the right hand pass the spindle through the hub and replace and tighten the off-side spindle nut. Deflect the telescopic forks several times to "centre" the near-side leg on the spindle. Do not over tighten the pinch stud nut on the near-side fork slider end. The lug on the fork end can be broken if this stud is over tightened. Finally re-connect and adjust the front-brake cable. See also page 122 (last paragraph).

Removing Quickly-detachable Rear Wheel (1955–63 Spring-frame Models). First place the motor-cycle on its centre stand. Slacken (1955–8) the bolt located at the rear on each tubular member to which the detachable rear-portion of the mudguard is attached. Also loosen the two bolts holding the two portions of the mudguard together. Disconnect the snap connector provided in the lead to the stop-tail lamp. Now remove the detachable rear-portion of the rear mudguard.

On 1959–63 models a deep section one-piece rear mudguard is fitted. To facilitate rear wheel removal it is desirable to lay some suitable packing (e.g. wood blocks) beneath the centre stand so as to lift the rear wheel a greater distance from the ground.

Referring to Fig. 61, disconnect the speedometer drive by unscrewing the cable gland-nut (5) and withdrawing the end of the driving cable from the speedometer-drive gearbox (4). Next remove the nut (11) and washer (12) from the near side of the hub spindle (7). Do not disturb the nut (8) which secures the speedometer gearbox (4). Withdraw the hub spindle (7), by means of its short tommy-bar, together with the distance collar (6), which will fall away as the spindle is withdrawn. Then ease the hub sideways from the drilled holes on the brake-drum wall (1955–6 models), or ease the rubber-sleeved pins on the hub from the tubular bosses on the brake-drum wall (1957–63 models). The rear wheel is then free to be withdrawn from the machine which should be leaned at an angle (1959–63 models).

To Replace Quickly-detachable Rear Wheel (1955–63 Spring-frame Models). Follow the removal procedure in reverse. Referring to Fig. 61, offer up the quickly-detachable wheel, insert the hub spindle (7) *without* the distance collar (6); engage the holes or tubular bosses in the brake-drum wall, with the hub driving-pins; hold the wheel in its normal position; withdraw the hub spindle. Then insert the distance collar and replace the hub spindle. When tightening the nut on the near-side of the spindle, make sure that the opposite end of the spindle contacts the secondary chain adjuster-screw, to ensure correct wheel alignment. This should be correct if the chain adjuster-screws have not been disturbed. If in any doubt, check the wheel alignment (*see* page 92); also check the adjustment of the rear brake (*see* page 96).

When replacing the rear wheel, make sure that the speedometer-drive dogs engage properly before tightening the cable gland-nut (5). Defer tightening the nut (8) locating the speedometer-drive gearbox (4) until the

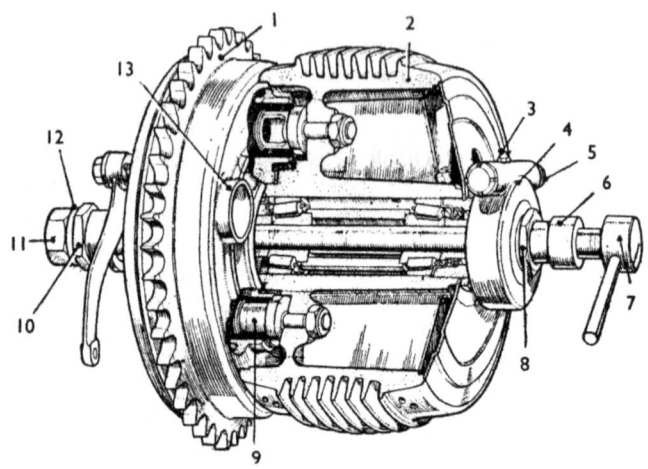

FIG. 61. DETAILS OF LIGHT-ALLOY HUB ASSEMBLY USED ON 1955–63 SPRING-FRAME MODELS WITH QUICKLY-DETACHABLE REAR WHEEL

On 1955–6 models the brake-drum wall has drilled holes instead of the tubular bosses shown; these bosses engage rubber-sleeved pins on the light-alloy hub.

(*By courtesy of "Motor Cycle"—London*)

KEY TO FIG. 61

1. Brake drum and sprocket.
2. Full-width light-alloy hub.
3. Grease nipple for 4.
4. Speedometer-drive gearbox.
5. Gland nut for speedometer-drive cable.
6. Distance collar.
7. Hub spindle.
8. Nut locating 4.
9. Rubber-sleeved driving pins on 2.
10. Nut securing brake cover plate.
11. Nut on spindle end.
12. Washer for 11.
13. Tubular bosses to engage pins 9.

driving cable has been connected up, and the hub-spindle nut (11) has been tightened. Also make sure that the brake cover-plate anchorage is correct (*see* Fig. 62).

To Remove Quickly-detachable Rear Wheel (1964–5 Models). Because a deep section one-piece rear mudguard is fitted it is desirable to lay some suitable packing (e.g. wood blocks) beneath the centre stand so as to lift the rear wheel a greater distance from the ground.

Remove the three rubber grummets from the off-side of the rear hub

GENERAL MAINTENANCE

and then with a box or socket spanner remove the three sleeve nuts which secure the rear hub to the brake drum. Unscrew and remove the right-hand portion of the wheel spindle. Remove on the same side the distance piece and speedometer-drive gearbox, and allow the latter to hang on its cable. Now withdraw the rear hub from the driving studs on the brake drum by pulling it to the off-side. By inclining the machine the rear wheel can then be lifted clear of the motor-cycle.

If it is desired to remove the brake drum, take off the hand adjuster

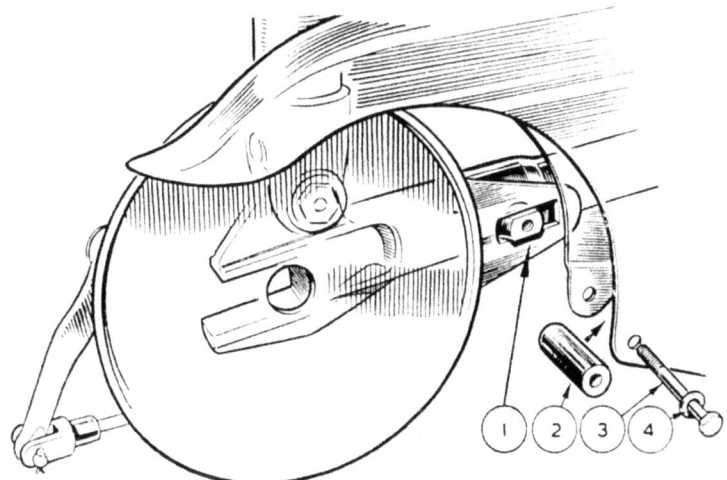

FIG. 62. THE REAR BRAKE COVER PLATE ANCHORAGE (1955–63 SPRING-FRAME MODELS)

KEY TO FIG. 62

1. Brake-anchorage boss.
2. Distance sleeve.
3. Anchorage bolt.
4. Washer.

from the rear brake rod and remove the secondary chain. Then unscrew the nut securing the dummy spindle and pull clear the brake drum.

To Replace Quickly-detachable Rear Wheel (1964–5 Models). Position the rear wheel under the mudguard and turn the brake drum (left in place) by hand so that one of the three driving studs is approximately in line with the pivoted fork. This assists in getting the bearing boss on the hub past the other two studs and fitting the wheel hub to the rear brake drum.

Fit and tighten the three sleeve nuts and replace the rubber grommets. Fit the speedometer-drive gearbox, being sure that its driving dogs properly engage with the slots in the hub bearing lock ring. Position the distance piece and fit on the off-side the right-hand position of the wheel spindle. Tighten the spindle firmly.

To Remove Rear Wheel (Not Quickly-detachable Type). First disconnect the rear brake rod by removing the split pin and yoke end pin. Also remove the connecting link of the secondary chain. Lay a sheet of paper beneath the chain to prevent its contamination with dirt. Next remove the bolt which passes through the rear brake anchor lug and the secondary chain guard. Be careful not to lose the distance piece between the chain guard.

Now disconnect the speedometer-drive cable from its drive. Loosen several turns the nut on the rear wheel spindle and pull the wheel to the off-side until the brake plate clears the anchor boss on the frame. Then remove the secondary chain from its sprocket and withdraw the rear wheel, inclining the motor-cycle at an angle to assist withdrawal under the silencer.

To Replace Rear Wheel (Not Quickly-detachable Type). Replace the rear wheel in the reverse order of that necessary for removal. Make sure that the rear brake cover-plate is properly anchored (*see* Fig. 62). Before tightening the rear wheel spindle nut, position the speedometer drive and connect the speedometer cable. While tightening the rear wheel spindle nut apply pressure to the rear brake pedal so as to centralize the brake shoes. A final hint: be sure that the closed end of the chain link spring clip faces the direction of chain travel.

Wheel Bearing Adjustment. 1964–5 hubs have ground ball bearings with no adjustment. It is advisable very occasionally to check the adjustment of the 1955–63 bearings and rectify it if necessary. The roller bearings of both wheels should be adjusted so that a slight amount of end-play (approximately 0·002 in.) can be felt. Should no end-play be present, there is an appreciable risk of the roller bearings becoming damaged during running; 0·002 in. bearing end-play represents a just perceptible end-play as felt at the rim. Rim rock should be just perceptible.

Adjusting the Roller Bearings (1955–63). To adjust the rear-wheel bearings, it is necessary to remove the wheel from the machine (*see* pages 119–122). On 1955–63 models the adjustment for both wheels is on the off-side.

To adjust the roller bearings of a front or rear wheel, loosen the lock-nut for the bearing adjusting-ring. Next tighten the bearing adjusting-ring until *all* play has been eliminated. Then slacken off the adjusting-ring exactly *one-half turn*. This should give about 0·002 in. end-play. Finally retighten the lock-nut, taking care to see that the adjusting-ring does not move in the process, and see that the hub cover plate (1955–63) is positioned to allow the grease gun to be applied to the grease nipple.

After Replacing the Front Wheel (1964–5). If stiffness of the telescopic front forks develops, loosen the spindle nut, work the forks up and down several times to align the fork tubes, and then retighten the spindle nut.

GENERAL MAINTENANCE 123

Dismantling Front Hub (1964–5). The journal hub bearings are packed with grease during initial assembly and this should suffice for at least 10,000 miles. Subsequently about every 10,000 miles dismantle the hub and repack the bearings with suitable grease (*see* page 23). To dismantle the front hub remove the wheel (*see* page 117) and then use the following procedure.

First remove the brake cover plate, complete with brake-shoe assembly. Unscrew the bearing lock-plate on the near-side of the hub, using a peg spanner or punch. Appropriate holes are provided on the lock-plate. Should it resist removal, apply a little heat. Remove the felt sealing washer and the distance piece. To eject the bearing, use the wheel spindle as a drift through the brake side. A few light blows applied with a mallet should suffice to drive out the bearing until it is clear of the hub, and no more, as the other bearing goes into the hub while using the wheel spindle as a drift. Remove the wheel spindle, invert the wheel, and repeat the procedure to eject the double bearing, together with the large steel washer, the felt washer, and also the thin washer.

To Assemble the Front Hub (1964–5). After cleaning and repacking both ball bearings with suitable grease, press into the near-side of the hub the

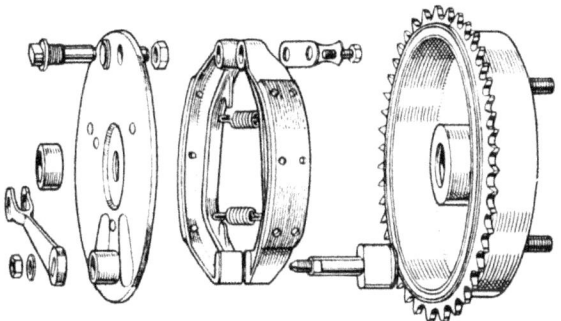

FIG. 63. EXPLODED VIEW SHOWING DETAILS OF 1964–5 REAR BRAKE-DRUM, BRAKE-SHOE ASSEMBLY, AND BRAKE ANCHOR-PLATE

The above comprise the near-side components of the 1964–5 quickly-detachable rear-wheel hub assembly shown dismantled in Fig. 64.

single bearing, fit the distance washer with its flat side against the bearing, the felt washer, and secure with the lock-plate. Invert the hub and insert the distance tube (small end first) against the bearing. Now enter the double-bearing square with the hub, insert the wheel spindle through both bearings, and drive home until the bearing abuts against the distance tube. Replace the smallest of the two washers, the felt washer, and then the large steel washer. With a suitable punch "peen" the hub material where it joins the washer in three equidistant positions to retain the washer.

Dismantling Rear Hub (1964–5). As in the case of the front hub, the rear hub has its journal ball bearings packed with grease during original assembly and this should last for at least 10,000 miles. At 10,000-mile intervals the wheel should be removed (*see* page 120), the hub dismantled, and the bearings repacked with suitable grease. To dismantle the rear hub, first remove the speedometer drive lock-ring (L.H. thread), take out the felt washer, and remove the distance piece. To eject the bearing use

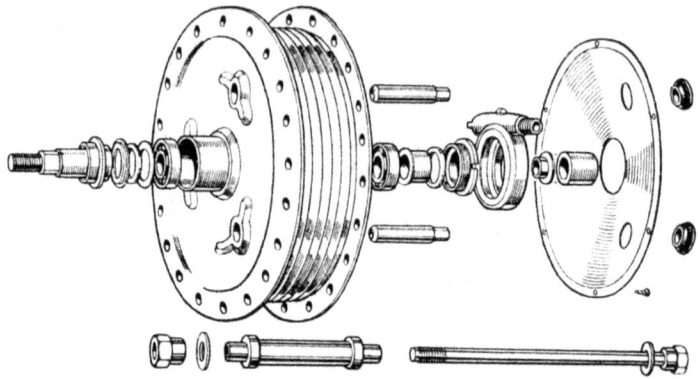

Fig. 64. Exploded View of 1964–5 Quickly-detachable Rear Wheel Hub Minus the Components Shown in Fig. 63.
Below are shown the two parts of the rear wheel spindle.

the wheel spindle with its washer, and also the distance piece provided between the speedometer drive and the rear fork end. Partially drive out the bearing until it abuts against the reduced diameter inside the hub. Remove the wheel spindle and, using a short length of steel tube with the outside diameter slightly smaller than the inside diameter of the bearing, drive out the bearing. Invert the wheel and then drift out the other bearing which will take with it the steel cup, felt washer, and the thin steel washer.

To Assemble the Rear Hub (1964–5). Deal with both bearings in the manner previously described. First fit the single-row bearing in the reverse order of removal. Note that when tightening the lock-ring care must be taken to avoid damaging the slots for the speedometer drive. Finally "peen" the hub dished washer to the hub.

INDEX

Air filter, 18
Alignment—
  headlamp, 20
  wheel, 92
Amal carburettor details, 10
Ammeter, 23
Automatic ignition-control, 66

Battery, maintenance, 23–7
Brake—
  adjustment, 94–7
  cover plate, 98
  lubrication, 54
  shoes, 97–9
Brakes, use of, 8
Brushes, commutator, 28
Bulb renewal, 22–3

Carbon deposits, removing, 77
Carburettor—
  adjustment, 14
  dismantling, 16
  settings, 14
Chain—
  dynamo, 29, 49, 103
  magneto, 49, 66
  primary, 51, 99
  secondary, 52, 101
Changing engine oil, 46
Cleaning—
  carburettor, 17
  chromium, 91
  contact-breaker, 65
  enamelled parts, 90
  engine, 59
  lamps, 23
  sparking plugs, 61
Clutch—
  adjustment, 105–8
  assembly, 111
  cable, 111
  plates sticking, 6
  shock-absorber, 104
  slip, 104

Commutator brushes, 28
Compensated voltage control, 29
Connexions, battery, 27, 38
Contact-breaker—
  gap, 63
  lubrication, 49
Controls, 3
Cover plate, brake, 98
Crankcase—
  filter, 46
C.V.C. unit, 29
Cylinder—
  barrel removal, 75, 81
  head removal, 75, 82

Decarbonizing, valve grinding, 72–85
Drain plug, crankcase, 46
Driving licence, 1
Dynamo—
  bearings, 49
  chain, 29, 31, 49, 103
  maintenance, 27–32
  removing, 30

Electrolyte level, 24, 25
Engine—
  lubrication, 39–49
  oils, suitable, 43
  shaft shock-absorber, 103
Exhaust-valve stem lubrication, 45

Felt element, removing, 47
Filters—
  carburettors, 18
  oil, 46
Front forks, "Roadholder", 56, 117
Front forks, "Teledraulic," 56, 115
Front-wheel removal, 117–19
Fuel consumption, excessive, 15

Gap—
  contact-breaker, 63
  sparking plug, 60–3
Gauze filters, oil tank, 46

126   THE BOOK OF THE A.J.S.

Gear—
　change indicator, 6
　changing, 5–8
Gearbox lubrication, 49
Grease gun, use of, 53
Grinding-in valves, 78

HANDLEBAR—
　adjustment, 114
　controls, 3
Harsh transmission, 103
Headlamps, 20–3
Hills, negotiating, 8
Horn adjustment, 33
H.T. cable, 66

IGNITION timing, 67–70
Illumination, correct, 20
Inlet-valve stem lubrication, 45
Insurance, 1

JET-NEEDLE wear, 17

KICK-STARTER, use of, 4

LIGHT unit, removing, 22
Lighting switch, 20
Lubrication—
　chart, 25
　engine, 39–49
　motor-cycle, 49–57

MAGNETIC crankcase-filter, 46
Magneto—
　bearings, 48
　chain, 49, 66
　timing, 67
"Monobloc" carburettor, 10–17

NUTS and bolts, 91

OIL—
　circulation, 41, 45
　level, 44
　pump, 39, 45
　tank, 43, 44
Oil-bath—
　chain case, removing, 108–11
　inspection cap, 52

PETROL tank, 4, 73, 84–5
Pilot-air adjusting screw, 14
Pilot-jet obstruction, 15
Piston—
　removal, 5, 81
　rings, 75, 81
Preliminaries, 1
Primary chain, 51, 99
Push-rod adjustment, 72

QUICKLY-DETACHABLE rear wheel, 120–1

REAR lamps, 23
Rear suspension, 57, 117
Rear-wheel removal, 119–22
Registration licence, 1
Repairs and spares, 58
"Roadholder" front forks, 117
Rocker-box removal, 73, 83
Running-in advice, 9

SECONDARY chain, 52, 101
Shock-absorbers, 103, 104
Sidecar alignment, 93
Slipping clutch, 104
Slow-running adjustment, 14
Sparking plugs, 60–3
Specific gravity of electrolyte, 26
Speedometer-gearbox lubrication, 54
Stand lubrication, 55
Starting engine, 4
Steering head, 54, 114
Sticking clutch-plates, 6
Stopping procedure, 9
Stop-tail lamps, 23
Switch, lighting, 20

TANK filters, 42, 46
Tappet adjustment, 71
Taps, petrol, 4
"Tekall," 91
"Teledraulic" front forks, 56, 115
Terminals, battery, 27, 38
Throttle twist-grip stiff, 54
Timing—
　coil, 68
　magneto, 67
Tools, 59, 90

Topping-up battery, 24
Tuning Amal carburettor, 13–16
Twist-grip adjustment, 16
Tyre pressures, 91–2

VALVE springs, 79
Valve timing, 85–90
Valves, grinding-in, 78
Vent plugs, battery, 24
Voltage control, 29

WARMING-UP engine, 5
Wheel—
  alignment, 92
  bearing adjustment, 122
  hub lubrication, 53
  hubs, dismantling, 123–4
  removal, 117–22
Wiring—
  diagrams, 35–7
  system, 34

OTHER MOTORCYCLE MANUALS AVAILABLE IN THIS SERIES

AJS (BOOK OF) ALL MODELS 1955-1965:
350cc & 500cc Singles ~ Models 16,16S,18, 18S

ARIEL WORKSHOP MANUAL 1933-1951:
All single, twin & 4 cylinder models

ARIEL (BOOK OF) MAINTENANCE & REPAIR MANUAL 1932-1939:
LF3, LF4, LG, NF3, NF4, NG, OG, VA, VA3, VA4, VB, VF3, VF4, VG, Red Hunter LH, NH, OH, VH & Square Four 4F, 4G, 4H

BMW FACTORY WORKSHOP MANUAL R27, R28:
English, German, French and Spanish text

BMW FACTORY WORKSHOP MANUAL R50, R50S, R60, R69S:
Also includes a supplement for the USA models: R50US, R60US, R69US.
English, German, French and Spanish text

BSA PRE-WAR SINGLES & TWINS (BOOK OF) 1936-1939:
All Pre-War single & twin cylinder SV & OHV models through 1939
150cc, 250cc, 350cc, 500cc, 600cc, 750cc & 1,000cc

BSA SINGLES (BOOK OF) 1945-1954:
OHV & SV 250cc, 350cc, 500cc & 600cc, Groups B, C & M

BSA SINGLES (BOOK OF) 1955-1967:
B31, B32, B33, B34 and "Star" B40 & SS90

BSA 250cc SINGLES (BOOK OF) 1954-1970:
B31, B32, B33, B34 and "Star" B40 & SS90

BSA TWINS (BOOK OF) 1948-1962:
All 650cc & 500cc twins

DUCATI OHC FACTORY WORKSHOP MANUAL:
160 Junior Monza, 250 Monza, 250 GT, 250 Mark 3, 250 Mach 1, 250 SCR & 350 Sebring

HONDA 250 & 305cc FACTORY WORKSHOP MANUAL:
C.72 C.77 CS.72, CS.77, CB.72, CB.77 [HAWK]

HONDA 125 & 150cc FACTORY WORKSHOP MANUAL:
C.92, CS.92, CB.92, C.95 & CA.95

www.VelocePress.com

HONDA 90 (BOOK OF) ALL MODELS UP TO 1966:
All 90cc variations including the S90, CM90, C200, S65, Trail 90 & C65 models

HONDA 50cc FACTORY WORKSHOP MANUAL: C.100

HONDA 50cc FACTORY WORKSHOP MANUAL: C.110

HONDA (BOOK OF) MAINTENANCE & REPAIR 1960-1966:
50cc C.100, C.102, C.110 & C.114 ~ 125cc C.92 & CB.92
250cc C.72 & CB.72 ~ 305cc CB.77

LAMBRETTA (BOOK OF) MAINTENANCE & REPAIR:
125 & 150cc, all models up to 1958, except model "48".

NORTON FACTORY TWIN CYLINDER WORKSHOP MANUAL 1957-1970: *Lightweight Twins:* 250cc Jubilee, 350cc Navigator and 400cc Electra and the *Heavyweight Twins:* Model 77, 88, 88SS, 99, 99SS, Sports Special, Manxman, Mercury, Atlas, G15, P11, N15, Ranger (P11A).

NORTON (BOOK OF) MAINTENANCE & REPAIR 1932-1939:
All Pre-War SV, OHV and OHC models: 16H, 16I, 18, 19, 20, 50, 55, ES2, CJ, CSI, International 30 & 40

SUZUKI 200 & 250cc FACTORY WORKSHOP MANUAL:
250cc T20 [X-6 Hustler] ~ 200cc T200 [X-5 Invader & Sting Ray Scrambler]

SUZUKI 250cc FACTORY WORKSHOP MANUAL: 250cc ~ T10

TRIUMPH (BOOK OF) MAINTENANCE & REPAIR 1935-1939:
All Pre-War single & twin cylinder models: L2/1, 2/1, 2/5, 3/1, 3/2, 3/5, 5/1, 5/2, 5/3, 5/4, 5/5, 5/10, 6/1, Tiger 70, 80, 90 & 2H. Tiger 70C, 3S & 3H, Tiger 80C & 5H, Tiger 90C, 6S, 2HC & 3SC, 5T & 5S and T100

TRIUMPH 1937-1951 WORKSHOP MANUAL (A. St. J. Masters):
Covers rigid frame and sprung hub single cylinder SV & OHV and twin cylinder OHV pre-war, military, and post-war models

TRIUMPH 1945-1955 FACTORY WORKSHOP MANUAL NO.11:
Covers pre-unit, twin-cylinder rigid frame, sprung hub, swing-arm and 350cc, 500cc & 650cc.

VESPA (BOOK OF) MAINTENANCE & REPAIR 1946-1959:
All 125cc & 150cc models including 42/L2 & Gran Sport

VINCENT WORKSHOP MANUAL 1935-1955:
All Series A, B & C Models

www.VelocePress.com

Please check our website:

www.VelocePress.com

for a complete
up-to-date list of
available titles

www.ingramcontent.com/pod-product-compliance
Lightning Source LLC
Chambersburg PA
CBHW060349190426
43201CB00043B/1839